"Suzanne has been a priceless source of wisdom in my life for many years. She is without question the best Enneagram teacher out there."

Nadia Bolz-Weber, author of *Accidental Saints*

"Suzanne Stabile understands that we are people made for relationships, and that we cannot understand who we are as individuals without better understanding others and how we relate to them. *The Path Between Us* offers a pathway to greater empathy, compassion, and wisdom in your relationships, and that is a gift for those who love you and for you too! I'm so grateful to have Suzanne as a friend and guide on so many of life's most important questions. With this book, Suzanne will guide you as well."

Michael Wear, author of *Reclaiming Hope*

"Few people can teach you the Enneagram with the genuine insight, humor, and potential for real growth and change better than Suzanne Stabile! Savor every page. You, your friends and family, and the universe will all benefit!"

Richard Rohr, Center for Action and Contemplation, Albuquerque, New Mexico

"If you've heard of the Enneagram but never understood it, the introduction to *The Path Between Us* is worth the price of this book; it provides the best short introduction to the Enneagram that I've ever seen. Each chapter is equally amazing. If you struggle to understand and get along with anyone— spouse, child, parent, boss, coworker, employee—you will find insights into what makes them tick and how you can forge a path of connection to them. In the process, you'll learn a lot about yourself as well. A treasure!"

Brian D. McLaren, author of *The Great Spiritual Migration*

"Since personality shapes our formation, many of us wonder how the Enneagram can help us belong in our closest relationships. We trust Suzanne Stabile to guide us in this discovery because of her wisdom and experience, and even more because of her generosity of spirit, social intelligence, and wholehearted love for people. *The Path Between Us* will help you be more compassionate toward the people in your life and yourself."

Mark Scandrette and Lisa Scandrette, authors of *Belonging and Becoming: Creating a Thriving Family Culture*

"Rarely have I read a book so perfectly titled. *The Path Between Us* helps the reader understand the sometimes complex interplay between Enneagram types. As a person who has long studied and tried to apply the Enneagram to my own relationships, this book is indeed the best guide I have found on the subject."

James Bryan Smith, author of *The Good and Beautiful God*

"After reading *The Path Between Us*, I felt like I understood my friends and family better than I have before, as well as the way I can be a better husband, father, friend, and coworker. This is a practical guide to understanding relationships through the Enneagram. This is a book you won't just read—you'll reference it for years to come."

Mike McHargue, author of *Finding God in the Waves*, host of *The Liturgists Podcast* and *Ask Science Mike*

"Suzanne has a terrific way of taking the complexities of an ancient, wonderful resource and making them practical and relevant for today. I love the tool, and I love Suzanne's way of presenting it. She is the best there is in illuminating the tangible benefits of the Enneagram."

Paul Rasmussen, senior minister at Highland Park United Methodist, Dallas

"While you're reading *The Path Between Us*, you'll be making a list in your head of all the loved ones you'll be blessing with this book. You'll want them to have it because this is deep wisdom about the human journey and yet, at the same time and as always, Suzanne offers it to us in such accessible and practical ways."

Burt Burleson, University Chaplain and Dean of Spiritual Life at Baylor University

"In a readable and engaging flow, *The Path Between Us* helps me to recognize my own contested corners of difficulty as I relate to people I love and cherish. I appreciate the direct language that Suzanne Stabile uses; she never minces words and she illustrates the truths of each person through the warmth of stories people tell about themselves. You can't giggle in print, but Suzanne clearly delights in the variety of human perspectives across the Enneagram. Her enthusiasm and delight are contagious; she is the Oprah of the Enneagram."

Suzii Paynter, executive coordinator of the Cooperative Baptist Fellowship

THE
PATH
BETWEEN
US

**AN ENNEAGRAM JOURNEY TO
HEALTHY RELATIONSHIPS**

SUZANNE STABILE

IVP Books

An imprint of InterVarsity Press
Downers Grove, Illinois

InterVarsity Press
P.O. Box 1400, Downers Grove, IL 60515-1426
ivpress.com
email@ivpress.com

InterVarsity Press® is the book-publishing division of InterVarsity Christian Fellowship/USA®, a movement of students and faculty active on campus at hundreds of universities, colleges, and schools of nursing in the United States of America, and a member movement of the International Fellowship of Evangelical Students. For information about local and regional activities, visit intervarsity.org.

All Scripture quotations, unless otherwise indicated, are taken from The Holy Bible, New International Version®, NIV®. Copyright © 1973, 1978, 1984, 2011 by Biblica, Inc.™ Used by permission of Zondervan. All rights reserved worldwide. www.zondervan.com. The "NIV" and "New International Version" are trademarks registered in the United States Patent and Trademark Office by Biblica, Inc.™

Some names and identifying information in this book may have been changed to protect the privacy of individuals.

Cover design: David Fassett
Interior design: Daniel van Loon and Jeanna Wiggins
Images: people walking: © Ricardo Dias /EyeEm / Getty Images
wavy line background: © Kalisson / iStock / Getty Images
Author photo: Courtney Perry

ISBN 978-0-8308-4642-9 (print)
ISBN 978-0-8308-7606-8 (digital)

Printed in the United States of America ∞

InterVarsity Press is committed to ecological stewardship and to the conservation of natural resources in all our operations. This book was printed using sustainably sourced paper.

Library of Congress Cataloging-in-Publication Data

Names: Stabile, Suzanne, author.
Title: The path between us : an Enneagram journey to healthy relationships /
Suzanne Stabile.
Description: Downers Grove : InterVarsity Press, 2018. | Includes
bibliographical references.
Identifiers: LCCN 2018011729 (print) | LCCN 2018017312 (ebook) | ISBN
9780830876068 (eBook) | ISBN 9780830846429 (hardcover : alk. paper)
Subjects: LCSH: Enneagram. | Personality. | Interpersonal relations.
Classification: LCC BF698.35.E54 (ebook) | LCC BF698.35.E54 S73 2018 (print)
| DDC 155.2/6—dc23
LC record available at https://lccn.loc.gov/2018011729

P 23 22 21 20 19 18 17 16 15 14 13 12 11

Y 36 35 34 33 32 31 30 29 28 27 26 25 24 23 22 21 20

For Giuseppe

The path between us defines the goodness of the life we share.
I love you with all of my heart.

For our children and those they love

Joey and Billy, Jenny and Cory, Joel and Whitney, B.J. and Devon

For our grandchildren

Will, Noah, Sam, Elle, Joley, Piper, Jase

For Richard Rohr OFM

Who taught me the Enneagram

For Sheryl Fullerton

Who taught me how to write about it

CONTENTS

Introduction
PAGE 1

9s
Risking Conflict
for Connection
PAGE 39

8s
Vulnerability Is
Not Weakness
PAGE 15

1s
Things Could
Always Be Better
PAGE 59

7s
It's All Good
PAGE 165

2s
Your Feelings
or Mine?
PAGE 77

6s
Question
Everything
PAGE 146

3s
Being Everyone
but Myself
PAGE 93

5s
My Fences
Have Gates
PAGE 128

4s
Go Away but
Don't Leave
PAGE 110

Conclusion
PAGE 183

Acknowledgments
PAGE 185

Notes
PAGE 189

THE ENNEAGRAM IS A JOURNEY

*J*oseph Stabile is the best person I know—he's good all the way through. We've shared life now for more than thirty years. Even so, there are still times when his actions leave me wondering if I will ever fully understand his way of being in the world.

A few years ago on a flight from New York to Dallas, we were seated in the middle of the main cabin watching strangers as they looked for a place to put their luggage in the already full overhead bins. The last couple to board included a gentle-looking older man carrying his suitcase in front of his body, peeking around it frequently to check for empty seats. His wife followed close behind, looking a bit frightened by all that was going on: there weren't two seats together, their suitcase would not fit under the seat, and there was no other space for it in the cabin. The flight attendant tried to get their attention, but neither one responded. It was clear they didn't speak English, so the flight attendant managed the situation the way many of us would—by simply talking louder.

Since Joe is bilingual I thought he could help, so I nudged him and pointed out the obvious communication problem. In fact, I was heavily invested in the prospect of his engagement—all to no avail. He insisted that the flight attendant could figure it out. And he was right. She took the gentleman's suitcase to the front, someone graciously gave up a seat so the couple could sit together, and my husband was content as we prepared for take-off.

Everyone was okay . . . everyone except *me.*

I communicate well, verbally *and* nonverbally. So even though nothing more was said right then, Joe knew that all was not well in his world because all was not well in mine. And since he's never one to work out things in public—and I'm not one who usually lets things go—we both knew it was only a matter of time.

We got home, settled in, went to bed, and greeted the next day with full schedules. But that next night at dinner I said, "You know that I think you are the best human being on the planet, and that's still true. But I want you to explain to me why you wouldn't help that couple on the airplane when they obviously needed a translator."

And then my husband, who is such a Nine, responded: "Honestly, it never occurs to me that I should help. I see that they are struggling, but I just don't think about getting involved."

I found myself, again, aware of the significant difference in the ways Joe and I see the world. I replied as a Two, "I *always* know who needs help, and I usually know what they need. I'm just not always equipped to offer assistance."

This story (and a thousand more like it) is the reason I wrote this book. All relationships—those that truly matter and even those that don't—require translation. And if our interest in relational growth and transformation is sincere, then the Enneagram is one of the most helpful translation tools available.

THE BEAUTY OF THE ENNEAGRAM

I am what is often called a "people person." Quite frankly, I find other people fascinating and I like them. Almost all of them. I like to talk to them and shake hands or hug or pat them on the back. At the same time, every person I know is a mystery to me—not so much in how they appear, though that in itself is miraculous. The thing I find captivating is that we all *behave* so differently.

However, in my experience there are two things we have in common: we all want to belong, and we all want our lives to have meaning. But finding belonging and meaning are dependent on our ability to build and maintain relationships—with people who are like us, and often with those who are not.

Some things about the way we do life change over time, but other things stay the same, and there's seemingly not much we can do about it. We are often confronted with the reality that other people and how they view the world may never make any sense. Keeping in mind that none of us can change how we see, we are left with the option of trying to adjust *what we do* with how we see.

The Enneagram teaches us that there are nine different ways of experiencing the world and nine different ways of answering these basic questions about life: *Who am I? Why am I here?* and *Why do I do the things I do?* How we build and maintain relationships varies significantly from one number to another. Looking through the lens of the Enneagram makes it possible to better understand ourselves and others, increase our acceptance and compassion, and navigate the paths between us.

This book will help in understanding how each of the nine Enneagram numbers sees the world, how they make sense of what they see, how they decide what to do, and how all of that affects how they relate to others. Of course, because this is a book about relationships, it won't be tidy—human interaction can be unpredictable and messy. Sometimes we get it right and other times we're dead wrong. The good news is that with the help of the Enneagram, we can all do better.

THE NUMBERS

The chapters that follow are written *about* each number and include helpful tips *for* that number as they look at their own relationships. Because these chapters detail the ways a specific number interacts with other numbers, general knowledge about the Enneagram will be helpful. This section offers a brief refresher on the basics. If you haven't read *The Road Back to You*, please do—it's a great introduction to the Enneagram and the perfect companion for this book.

1s are called *Perfectionists*, but they don't like that title. They struggle with anger but they turn it in on themselves so it becomes resentment. Ones have a hard time believing that they are good enough or worthy because of a constant inner voice that finds fault with everything they do, so they settle for being right or correct. Ones have a judging/comparing mind. They notice error that others don't see and they often feel a personal responsibility to correct it. They believe every step of a task should be done correctly, so they give their best, do their best, offer their best, and they expect the same from others.

2s are called *Helpers* or *Givers*. They need to be needed. Twos give a lot, sometimes for altruistic reasons and sometimes in order to receive in return, although it is usually a subconscious motivation. When Twos enter a room their attention automatically turns to others and asks, "How are you doing?" "What do you need?" "How can I be helpful?" Their motivation is to build relationships by sensing and meeting the needs of others.

3s are called *Performers*. They need to be and be seen as successful, efficient, and effective. Threes have trouble reading feelings—their own feelings as well as the feelings of others. Threes often hide their anger, fear, sadness, disappointment, and embarrassment until they are alone to deal with them. They like to set short-term and long-term goals and they usually achieve them. They motivate the rest of us to do things we might never have imagined. And when we win, they win.

4s are the most complex number on the Enneagram. They are called *Romantics,* and their need is to be both unique and authentic at the same time. Fours believe something is missing in their lives and they won't be okay until they find it. They are comfortable with melancholy and often get energy from what is tragic. They are the only number on the Enneagram that can bear witness to pain without having to fix it. Because they value authenticity and abhor disingenuousness, Fours naturally elicit more depth in their encounters with others.

5s are called *Observers* or *Investigators.* Fives want adequate resources so they never have to depend on someone else. They are the most emotionally detached of all the numbers. This kind of detachment means that they can have a feeling and let it go. They manage fear by gathering information and knowledge. Fives have a limited, measured amount of energy for every day so they are careful about what they offer to others and when. It is extremely brave of them to show up for relationships because it costs them more than any other number.

6s are called *Loyalists*. They need to feel secure and certain, yet they have a lot of anxiety about possible future events, a world full of threats, and the hidden agendas of others. Sixes manage that anxiety with worst-case scenario planning, order and rules, plans, and the law. They don't want or need to be the star—they simply do their part and hope everyone else will too. With their loyalty and steadfastness, Sixes are the glue that holds together all of the organizations we treasure and belong to. They are more concerned about the common good than any other number.

7s are called *Epicures* or *Enthusiasts*. They take delight in the best possibilities. They need to avoid pain, and they quickly reframe any negative into a positive. Sevens fool themselves into believing they have a full range of emotions, when in fact they live most of life on the happy side—life is to be experienced and enjoyed. This means repetition is not desirable and routine is a turnoff. Sevens are also masters of denial, managing fear by diffusing it. Yet they have a special way of uplifting people around them. Truthfully, we would have a lot less fun in our lives without them.

8s are called the *Boss* or *Challenger*. They are independent thinkers who tend to see everything in extremes: good or bad, right or wrong, friend or foe. Anger is their emotion of choice, but it doesn't last long. While Eights don't invite forthrightness, they want and respect it. Their focus is outside of themselves and they are always for the underdog. Eights are passionate! They have more energy than any number, giving everything they have to what they are doing or what they believe in, and engaging most with people who are willing to go all out.

9s are called *Peacemakers* or *Mediators*. They are the least complex number on the Enneagram. They have the least energy of all the types because they try to keep in anything that would cause conflict and keep out anything that would steal their peace. Nines are the most stubborn number. They manage their anger by being passive-aggressive. They have the gift and the problem of seeing two sides to everything, so they are prone to procrastination and indecision. In relationships, Nines are loyal and like to be close. They are self-forgetting, setting aside their own needs and agendas to merge with others.

> The Enneagram offers a unique perspective for accepting what is.

THE ENNEAGRAM SYSTEM

The Enneagram is unique in what it offers as we make our way from who we are to who we hope to be. As you begin this journey, here's an overview of the dynamics of the Enneagram.

TRIADS. Within the system of the Enneagram there are three ways of meeting the world: feeling, thinking, or doing. The nine numbers are divided among those three ways, known as triads, and your triad is determined by how you encounter information or situations. Twos, Threes, and Fours are part of the Heart Triad, where feelings dominate. The Head Triad includes Fives, Sixes, and Sevens and is dominated by thinking. Doing is dominant for the Gut Triad, which includes Eights, Nines, and Ones.

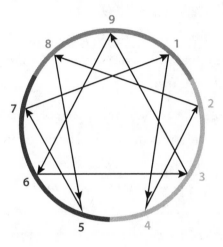

WINGS, STRESS, AND SECURITY. Each number on the Enneagram has a dynamic relationship with four other numbers: the two numbers on either side as well as the two at the other ends of the arrows in the diagram above. These four other numbers can be seen as resources that give you access to different patterns of behavior. While your core motivation and number never change, your behavior can be influenced by and can even make you look like another of these numbers. Mature students of the Enneagram can learn to move around the circle, using these four auxiliary ways of behaving as needed.

The four dynamic numbers are the following:

Wing numbers. These are the numbers on either side of your number, and they have the capacity to significantly impact behavior. For example, a Four with a Three wing is more outgoing than a Four with a Five wing, who is more introverted and withdrawing. Wings, in general, affect behavior when dominant, but have no effect on core motivation. Understanding the degree to which you lean into one wing or the other is important in understanding your own personality.

Stress number. This is the number your personality draws on when you are stressed, indicated by the arrow pointing away from your number on the diagram above. For example, in stress Sevens draw from One behavior. They can become less easygoing and adopt more black-and-white thinking. Your stress number is not necessarily a negative move—you need the behavior of the number you go to in stress to take care of yourself.

Security number. Just as you draw from one number when stressed, you also draw on the behavior of another number when you're feeling secure. This is indicated by the arrow pointing toward your number on the diagram above. For example, Sevens draw from Five behavior when they're feeling secure, letting go of their need for excess and embracing a less-is-more mentality. All numbers need the behavior available in security to experience holistic healing.

STANCES. In everyday language, *stance* describes how we stand or carry ourselves. It's much the same in the Enneagram: stance indicates a posture or attitude that is a habitual, patterned way of responding to experiences. It's the default mode for how a number behaves. In each chapter I will offer you a bit of insight as to how the stance of the number relates to how he or she navigates relationships.

The Aggressive Stance (Threes, Sevens, Eights). These people are happy to be in charge of others, and they put their agendas first. They are seen as standing independently and, at times, as moving against others. Their orientation to time is the future.

The Dependent Stance (Ones, Twos, Sixes). These people are very concerned with others' expectations so they are loyal and dependable. They are seen as moving toward others, and their orientation to time is the present.

The Withdrawing Stance (Fours, Fives, Nines). These people are slow to act because they are often shy or introverted. They are seen as moving away from others, and their orientation to time is the past.

A WORD OF ADVICE

I know you will be tempted to go straight to the chapter about your number and read that first, followed by the numbers of the people you are closest to. I might do the same thing. But I would encourage you to read the *whole* book. You will find information about your number as you relate to the other numbers included in every chapter. Your next step will be to read and use *The Path Between Us Study Guide*, perhaps with another person or in a group.

It is my hope that this book will help you make all of your relationships better, not just a chosen few. But I would be remiss if I didn't mention some things we should all watch out for when applying the wisdom of the Enneagram to our relationships.

> Your understanding of *who you are* affects every relationship you enter into and try to maintain.

It's important to remember that the Enneagram is not a static system: we are all moving from healthy, through average, to unhealthy, and back again. In my experience, most of us spend our time somewhere in the high-average range. We often respond to life from a healthy place, and during challenging times we probably react in unhealthy ways. So this book primarily depicts how we respond to others when we're in the average to healthy range.

We also need to keep in mind that there are many variations of each number. Those variations result from whether you are introverted or extroverted; whether you are, at that moment, in a healthy, average, or unhealthy space; whether you are social, one-to-one focused, or self-preserving; whether your orientation to time is the present, the past, or the future;

and how familiar you are with the Enneagram as well as other tools for personal and spiritual growth.

Finally, since we are talking about relationships, there are a few key interpersonal principles to keep in mind as you read. First, please don't use your Enneagram number as an excuse for your behavior. Second, don't use what you've learned about the other numbers to make fun of, criticize, stereotype, or in any way disrespect them. Ever. Third, it would be great if you would spend your energy observing and working on yourself as opposed to observing and working on others. And going forward, I hope you will share my desire that we all grow in our ability to accept, love, and walk beside one another on the path with loads of compassion and respect.

IT'S WORTH THE WORK

Recently Joe and I were on another flight and were seated in the second exit row. In the row in front of and across from us, the flight attendant was asking a passenger if he spoke English. He said, "No," so she asked again. And again he shook his head and said, "No." Since she continued, in English, to explain to the passenger that he could not sit in the exit row unless he spoke English, he continued to engage with her, attempting to understand what she was saying.

In an effort to be respectful of what Joe taught me about Nines the last time we traveled together, I remained silent.

Then, just as I buckled my seat belt, Joe unbuckled his. Noticing the struggle, he stepped over me into the aisle and, in Spanish, explained to the gentleman that he would need to trade seats with the woman in front of him because of an airline requirement that everyone in the exit row speak English.

The man got up to move. Smiling, he thanked Joe for helping him. When my thoughtful, bilingual husband returned to his seat, the woman behind us reached over the top of her seat, patted him on the shoulder, and thanked him for being so kind and so very helpful.

When we are able to see ourselves as we are, and as we can be, it's a beautiful thing.

8s

VULNERABILITY IS
NOT WEAKNESS

*M*elissa called and asked if we could talk about a problem at work, so I suspected it was in regard to her relationship with a colleague at her new job. The head of recruiting at a high-tech startup, Melissa is smart, creative, and very successful. She's a good leader, but like other Eights she often struggles in relationships with her co-workers. Eights function best when they can choose who they work with, but Melissa inherited her staff when she joined the company. From earlier conversations, I knew that she would not have chosen Emily.

Melissa had previously told me how tired she was of hearing Emily whine about the database system. "Instead of whining, why can't she just learn it!" Melissa usually worked fifty-five hours a week and was angry that Emily struggled to work forty, often missing work-related events for her aging mother's doctor appointments, her granddaughter's ballet recitals, and other personal conflicts.

When I answered the call from Melissa, she was already operating at an increased volume, as is typical for Eights. Like other Eights, who seldom have time for or any interest in small talk, she jumped right in. "It's about Emily. We just completed her six-month performance review. I started by asking her if she had anything she wanted to talk about before we discussed her evaluation. I thought that was such a great way to start—you know, kind of personal."

But Melissa was not prepared for what she heard next. With a shaky voice, Emily said, "I don't think you respect me. You are always so impatient and demanding. Sometimes I even feel bullied by you. Other people I have talked to said they have felt that too."

I could tell by her tone that Melissa was still angry, but I also knew she was hurt. I asked how she responded to Emily.

"Well," she said, "I paused and then asked some questions."

"What kind of questions?"

"I wanted her to give me objective proof for her feelings, so I asked her what happened to make her feel that way. I told her I had been very honest with her about my expectations and her responsibilities. I tried to explain to her that our department is very important to this phase of building the business and that we have a responsibility to recruit the right people for crucial positions or the company will fail."

There was a long pause, and then Melissa asked me very sincerely, "Suzanne, why can't people *just do their jobs*?"

What's Going on Here?

Which person in this story do you identify with most? Why?

Is Melissa a bully? Why or why not?

What does Emily really want from Melissa?

How can the Enneagram explain what's happening here?

Through the lens of the Enneagram, this story is about so much more than an aggressive boss and an intimidated or ineffective employee. It's about two people who see the job and their working relationship—and the world—from completely different perspectives. Melissa is an Eight. Emily is not. Melissa thought she was encouraging Emily to fulfill her professional responsibilities, so she was blindsided by Emily's emotional outburst. Although they managed to finish the performance review, Melissa shared with me that she had no confidence that things would change. Eventually, Emily asked to be transferred.

Most Enneagram numbers broker peace with others as they go through the day—bridging emotional distance with a quick exchange, observation, or compliment before each going their own way. Unfortunately, Eights don't feel the obligation that prompts this kind of relational cleanup, so they usually move on to the next thing. It can feel like Eights don't care about us, but the fact is they simply aren't thinking about us—they are thinking about what needs to be done next.

In this story about Melissa and Emily, like so many stories that make up our days, we know what happened but we don't know why. The Enneagram helps us understand the dynamics, motivations, and experiences of all nine numbers and their interactions and relationships with one another.

THE WORLD OF EIGHTS

An Eight's first response to anything is "What am I going to *do*?" This can be tricky in relationships because many other people initially ask, "What do I *think*?" or "What do I *feel*?" Eights tend to get along very well with Threes and Sevens, who are also all about doing. These three numbers struggle with others who seem to be burdened by feelings or slow to respond because they think too long before they act.

In the context of relationships, doing as a first response often seems aggressive to other Enneagram numbers who are more oriented toward thinking or feeling. So Eights need to stop long enough to consider that for some,

Every number avoids something.

thinking must come before acting, and for others, feelings determine what action will be taken and when. This isn't just a matter of preference—it has to do with how we see. For example, Fives and Sixes think it's outrageous and irresponsible to take such quick action since they are so sure people need to evaluate multiple options and outcomes first.

But any kind of pause is difficult for Eights since they want to have control over what's happening inside of them and in the world. Sometimes Eights act too quickly, leaving no room for other perspectives or to allow others to offer what they have to give. Even so, people still look to Eights to make decisions and lead, expecting them to slow their pace, explain the plan, and ask for suggestions. With a focus on doing, none of that would occur to an Eight. Todd Dugas, an Eight who serves as the executive director of a recovery center, explains it this way:

> I used to feel resentment toward my staff because they were not doing their part. And then when I thought about it, I realized I never trained them or told them what I really wanted. I just gave them the basics and expected that they would expand on that somehow. Maybe that's because sitting down, interacting with them, and really having a conversation was a struggle. I also struggled with other staff members who were *just* barely doing their job. I used to get rid of those people all the time.

Eights need to pay attention when they move so quickly in a relationship that others can't keep up. Others will often go

Eights in average or below space may be tempted to get even with people who have treated them or others unjustly.

8

along, but it's likely because they don't feel like they have a choice. And this often results in resentment.

One Eight said: "The biggest misunderstandings we have at home are centered around times when I have expectations of others that I haven't clearly articulated. When they are not operating at the same speed or intensity as I am, I get really frustrated, really fast. Explaining what we are doing and why can be burdensome. But at times I need to include the others in my family plan." The truth is, when Eights choose inclusion it requires very little time and the payoff is significant: it alleviates misunderstanding and creates significant connections.

VULNERABILITY AND SELF-PROTECTION. Eights avoid vulnerability to protect themselves emotionally. As children, others made comments about them such as, "She's so bossy" or "He doesn't listen to anybody." As adults, they are often labeled as aggressive, so others frequently adopt a defensive stance in relationships with them, feeling a need to protect themselves in some way. The irony is that Eights also feel the need to protect themselves, but they do it by avoiding helplessness, weakness, and subordination.

In her now-famous TED talk on the subject of vulnerability, Brené Brown, a leading researcher and writer, said, "Vulnerability is the idea that in order for connection to happen we have to allow ourselves to be seen—really seen." Eights want to feel connected to those who are close to them as much as any other number. But they have a big problem:

one of the very few things they are afraid of is being exposed in moments of weakness, limitation, or indecision. If Brown is right and connection depends on our ability to be vulnerable, and being vulnerable suggests we are willing to be seen, then that relational motivation is key. I think Eights feel as exposed as the rest of us do at times. They just express it differently.

An Eight who is married and the mother of four explained her vulnerability in her family relationships:

> I will want to trust you with everything even though that is hard for me. I will be in your corner all the time. I will fight *for* you more than I will fight *with* you. I will surprise you with my mushy tears and maybe even eventually I won't try to cover them up. I will feel angry at you when you are being angry at me, and I'll have to work really hard to find the feelings underneath that. I will love you beyond reason and that might scare me in the beginning.

Although Eights can be vulnerable in close relationships, they always struggle with their discomfort of expressing softer feelings.

Despite their best efforts to protect themselves, Eights, like all of us, have experiences in life that they are not prepared for. In those times, when they feel emotionally exposed, Eights allow us to see them. If only briefly, we are given an opportunity to know them in a new way. In such moments, the Eights in my life have taught me that they are not intending to be aggressive—they are just trying to protect themselves.

When my daughter Joey was a little girl—six or seven years old—she would get up in the middle of the night to open and rewrap the Christmas packages under the tree that had her name on them. She did such a good job that it took us a couple of years to catch on. When we talked with her about it she explained that she didn't like surprises. "When I open my presents, I might cry or laugh or say the wrong thing. I don't like that. I want to know everything before it happens." Not knowing made her feel vulnerable. She is now nearly forty with children of her own, and she still wants to know everything before it happens.

Eights abhor weakness in themselves and those close to them, so if they can't distinguish between being vulnerable and being weak, they avoid both. But it's very difficult to be in a relationship with someone who can't or won't be vulnerable. It makes others feel as if their presence doesn't matter, like they don't have anything to offer, and that they could never be trustworthy enough. Good, solid relationships are built in vulnerable times, so Eights need to work on that confusion

> **8** Eights have good boundaries for protecting their own space, but may be unaware that they are getting into others' business.

about weakness and vulnerability by staying connected to others when they're down or when things don't line up, and then sharing with others what means the most, what frightens them the most, and what they consider most important.

In my experience, most Eights are old souls. They arrive on the planet with an unexpected wisdom that shows itself so gracefully you could almost miss it. They tell me that when they were little they were very uncomfortable around others who seemed to be weak and halfhearted, so they made the decision to be strong. Many of them take responsibility for themselves and others at a very early age because they are born leaders. But this chosen strength costs them their innocence. If you're an Eight, you will spend part of your adult life trying to regain your capacity to encounter the world without having to protect yourself from it. The ability to do that will come to you only in the context of safe relationships.

STANDING UP FOR THE UNDERDOG. Eights' preoccupation with self-protection means they are the best equipped to challenge oppressors and stand up for people who aren't as strong as they are. I love this about the Eights I know. Their concern about injustice and their belief that they are responsible for protecting the innocent is both powerful and gentle at the same time. However, Eights often miss out on what's in it for them; when Eights engage with those who are marginalized, they need to be aware that the giving can be mutual and relational.

Social awareness is the ability to pick up on the feelings of others and understand what life looks like from their point of view. This kind of awareness requires listening and observing. It's foundational for a respectful and meaningful exchange between two people even if the relationship is not ongoing. When Eights are busy getting things done on behalf of someone else, there's a good chance they are solving the problem without much social awareness. There's a delicate balance here that all numbers need to work on. Twos, for example, pay too much attention to being socially aware. But relationships are defined by the way two or more people are connected, so we need to be reminded that all relationships require a balance of give-and-take for both parties.

INTENSITY AND ANGER. In Enneagram wisdom, the Eight's passion is lust, which is best defined as intensity. They are all-in people full of high energy and an impatient drive toward action. When things don't line up or obstacles appear, Eights often respond with anger. Paradoxically, they believe anger has been helpful to them in making their way in the world, but I suspect Eights use anger to cover softer, more tender feelings. The problem seems to be, in part, that after a while they have trouble accessing any feelings *other than* anger, something that is often detrimental to their relationships.

When we remember the Eight's concerns about appearing to be weak, it makes sense that they would automatically mask sadness, fear, and vulnerability with anger as a way of protecting themselves. However, speaking for the other numbers on the Enneagram, Eight anger is often perceived as a barrier, not a boundary. The less aggressive types (Two, Four, Six, Nine) tend to be guarded in their encounters with Eights, and when that happens, the truth and authenticity Eights look for in relationships are less likely to become reality.

Wendi, a friend who is an Eight and teaches elementary school, told me about a debate she had with a colleague regarding the placement of kids in kindergarten and first grade classes. Wendi thought they had reached a consensus about what would be best for the children and that the problem was solved. When she found out their agreement had not been honored, she was very upset. She stormed down for an angry confrontation that left a huge rift in their relationship. But in the wake of her righteous anger, Wendi considered her actions:

> If I had waited and processed what was happening in a calm and thoughtful way before I talked to her, perhaps I could have presented my thoughts and feelings in a way that she could hear them. And if not, then at least I wouldn't have to reexamine my behavior afterwards. I'm learning to stop and think before I go talk to anyone when I am angry. I want to be respected and seen as level-headed and smart and wise and mature. Overreacting leaves me in a place of feeling like I need to justify my behavior.

Eights rarely regret confrontation. They rely on the energy they get from their need to be independent, but they often miss the reality that their aggression overshadows their intent.

The real problem is that lust, intensity, and anger masquerade as expressions of deep emotions, so Eights are fooled into believing that they are in touch with their feelings when that is often far from the truth. It takes an awareness of intention for Eights to recognize, feel, and then name their feelings.

DISCONNECTION FROM FEELINGS. Eights have an abundance of passion for everything and nothing in particular, often substituting intensity for other feelings such as joy or sadness or vulnerability or embarrassment. An encounter with tender feelings such as hurt or fear elicits a consistent and quick response of decisive action in order to feel strong again. Any sense of weakness or dependence is avoided at all cost. Problems arise because relationships thrive on *inter*dependence—frequent but unplanned mutuality between people who are in relation to one another. Eights need to realize that tender feelings are not a sign of weakness.

The illusion of control is shattered when Eights are confronted with feelings they can't repress. We've all seen it: a display of tenderness for someone close who is both fragile and strong, a love for one whose life is marginalized but whose response to life is not, a deep affection for another who overcomes indescribable odds with regularity. Eights aren't afraid to feel—they're afraid their feelings will betray them.

FEAR OF BETRAYAL. In my workshops, Eights talk a lot about being betrayed, frequently naming some of the people who have been disloyal to them. I listened to Eights tell these stories of betrayal for a long time before I began to say things like, "I wouldn't call that betrayal—don't you think it could have been a mistake?" Or, "I think that was a poor choice, but I wouldn't call it betrayal." When I reframe these events for Eights, they seem surprised. It doesn't occur to them that what they experience as betrayal might be something else, or might be very different if viewed from the other person's point of reference.

One afternoon at a family birthday party, I had a chance to talk about betrayal with Joey, our resident Eight. Sitting side by side, feet in the swimming pool with refreshing beverages in hand, I asked her to explain betrayal to me from her perspective. Her answer was simple: "I experience betrayal every day because people who don't know me make a judgment about who I am and then feed that judgment with their own feelings without ever making an effort to know me or connect with me in any way."

The last thing an Eight wants is to hurt someone they love. When they discover they have hurt you, their inner response is far from mechanical. Even if they maintain their composure, they suffer greatly and are devastated to learn they have taken advantage of your vulnerability in any way.

STRESS AND SECURITY

One of the strengths of the Enneagram is that it's not static like so many other systems of its kind, and yet it's predictable. Depending on where someone is on their journey and the way circumstances unfold, each number can be in the healthy, average, or unhealthy range. When Eights are healthy and at their best in relationships, they are positive, playful, and generous. They can be very accepting and willing to hang in there with whatever is going on. In this space they are committed, truthful, and supportive of others as long as others are committed to success.

We all have the same initial response to stress: we exaggerate behavior in our number.

At their most unhealthy, Eights are combative, possessive, arrogant, uncompromising, and quick to find fault. An Eight explained that the neediness of her children is something that really sets her off: "I tell my kids, get it together, guys. You are better than this. I didn't get four degrees to do your laundry. I'm raising men, not weak little boys. Take care of yourself!" However, Eights can learn to recognize that neediness in others is usually an attempt for connection, and that there is something to be gained by reaching back.

Excess in any number is not a good thing. Eights in stress respond with aggression, intensity, and palpable self-assurance. The primary defense mechanism of Eights is to deny all feelings that crop up from time to time. It pushes them to work harder and do more, when what they need to do is stop.

I think it's fair to say that what most of us experience as stressful—deadlines, confrontations, arguments, crises, the problematic behavior of others, or events that seem to be spinning out of control—Eights consider comfortable. They wade right into situations like these with excitement and resolve. One Eight explained, "I walk in like the Terminator, looking to identify friend or foe. Who is against me? Who is for me? That's how I protect myself. I want to look the part so nobody can control me. When I put on my highest heels, I'm 6'1", so I can look down on everyone in the room."

For the sake of our relationships it's important to acknowledge that some—perhaps most—Eights actually believe they can change reality to conform to their way of seeing things. Now as you're reading this, don't say to yourself, "That's crazy!" Remember

8s and Others

1s: Eights are committed and energetic like Ones, but they don't share the same focus: Ones generally focus on the problem, and Eights focus on the solution.

2s & 5s: Eights share a line with both Twos and Fives on the Enneagram, moving to Two in security and Five in stress. Eights need tenderness, affection, and awareness of the feelings of others from Twos. Eights need a Five's ability to move slowly, gathering necessary information before acting, as well as the ability to appreciate times when neutrality is of value.

3s & 7s: Eights do really well with Threes and Sevens because they all think fast, work hard, play hard, get a lot done, and are not prone to tender feelings. These three types are all oriented to the future and energetic in going after things, and make great coworkers and colleagues.

4s: Eights have a difficult time being present to the mood changes of a Four. But once Eights learn to allow for that they may discover that Eights and Fours actually have a lot in common: they are the most intense and passionate numbers on the Enneagram, and they are both committed to being honest regardless of cost.

6s: Eights have a hard time being patient enough to wait for Sixes. Sixes are methodical so they see things in real time, whereas Eights usually focus on the future. But when Eights listen to Sixes and wait for a response, it can be a win/win.

8s: Eights with Eights represent a lot of passion, so one of them will need to focus inward at times and responsibilities will need to be divided. Keep in mind that an Eight with a Seven wing is very different from an Eight with a Nine wing.

9s: An Eight can have a fascinating relationship with a Nine when both are mature and in healthy space. Nines need to have their own energy, agenda, and understanding of what is theirs to do; when Eights willingly and intentionally follow Nines, that can be a beautiful thing.

Eights think your way of seeing and doing things is crazy too. That's one of the reasons we need the Enneagram.

Eights deny their own limits, which is why they're either all in or not in at all. Unfortunately, without Enneagram knowledge or some life experience they deny others' limits too. Many Eights even deny that *there are limits*. The stress this causes takes its toll on them and on their relationships with others.

In stressful situations, male Eights simply refuse to stop. They expect more and more from themselves and from others, and anyone who can't keep up is suspect. If you live with or work with an Eight, then you know their anger can fill a room. It's daunting for people who are new to the experience. When male Eights fail, as they will at some point, they sometimes retreat, but more often they keep going and doing. I've heard many stories from male Eights who have been diagnosed with stress-related illnesses such as heart attacks and strokes because they couldn't accept that there is a time and a place for stopping.

When female Eights are highly stressed, they are bossy and strident. Their anger is unmistakable and they refuse to be appeased. But unlike their male counterparts, when they eventually hit the wall, they tend to slide down it, cry for a while, and go to bed. If they are fairly healthy, they might take their leave with a word about returning. If not, they leave no doubt in anyone's mind that they are angry and that they will be unavailable for an undisclosed amount of time.

Although Eights thrive on stress, that excess energy can reach a point of diminishing returns. When this happens, they intuitively draw from Fives and pull back from the world. That's a good thing. It offers space to think things through and reengage with life and others from a better place. When Eights are feeling secure they have access to some Two energy and behavior. That is good because, in this space, they connect emotionally with others in a way that allows for an exchange of tenderness that is often covered up by aggression.

LIMITATIONS IN RELATIONSHIPS

It would be a misunderstanding to think that Eights don't desire and value relationships—they do. But they don't need or have time for many relationships, so they aren't usually friends with coworkers. Keep in mind that Eights are collegial and good team players. It's just that meaningful social connections are usually lived out in other areas of their lives.

Eights prefer a few friendships with people who also value independence. To be friends with an Eight, you will need to be trustworthy and safe, and the relationship needs to be reliable but free of expectations. One of my apprentices says, "It is literally *impossible* for me to have a meaningful relationship with someone who doesn't have the self-confidence to stand up for themselves."

Many Eights experience a lack of balance that is the result of an overemphasis on doing and an unconscious habit of ignoring feelings—theirs and others'. But that focus on doing can cost them dearly.

As the oldest of three boys and the only Eight in his family, Jeff was well-suited for making decisions for his parents as they aged, but he didn't necessarily want to do it alone. Though Jeff wanted his brothers to be involved, as time passed, he had more and more responsibility and they had less. He assumed they couldn't or wouldn't do what needed to be done and ended up having his mother move in with him after her health declined.

Following the well-established family pattern, Jeff handled everything after his mother's death: he chose the funeral home and casket, wrote the obituary for the newspapers, and gave the eulogy. After the service, Jeff's twelve-year-old daughter asked why he never cried. In that moment of endings and beginnings and vulnerability, Jeff gathered her up and hugged her fiercely. But he couldn't tell her what he believed to be true: if he had let his emotions take over, there would have been no one to do what needed to be done in burying his mother. I think many Eights live a lifetime believing they must ignore their softer feelings in order to get the job done.

The truth is that what we see and the way we see also determine what we miss. I'm convinced that Eights have no idea how their unwillingness to be vulnerable affects other people. Eights don't know that their take-charge aggressiveness makes others feel like their presence is unimportant or unneeded. Eights don't realize that many of us take their lack of vulnerability to mean they don't trust us with who they really are, warts and all. Long-term, committed relationships are built, in part, by walking beside someone, neither leading nor following, in celebration and suffering.

Eights are usually in charge no matter where they are or who they're with. So it's important for them to remember that relationships are built on mutuality and collaboration, and both are easy to dismiss for those who are always in leadership mode. One of my favorite people, writer and pastor Nadia Bolz-Weber, once told me about how she had to be mindful of how much weight her opinion carries with her congregation at House for All Sinners and Saints:

> The way the church runs, we don't have a committee system . . . so everything is sort of "opt in." I'll say, "Who wants to have a liturgy guild meeting for Ash Wednesday

and the Sundays in Lent?" And whoever shows up is the liturgy guild that day. But in order for it to work, I have to be willing to let go of two things, which are control and predictability. You can't predict who will come . . . or if anyone will come. And I have to let go of control, meaning I have to allow them to participate. So, it's a very particular type of leadership. It's not "anything goes"—I'm still leading, I'm still holding that space. But, if somebody has an idea I have to check in with myself and I have to check in with the room. And I have to do it honestly. And I have to do it quickly. . . . I have to be responsible with the fact that my voice has a lot of weight. And it takes a bit of self-awareness, and I don't always do it right, but that's the stuff that ends up being hard. But if you do enough of your work you can manage it. You're not going to run roughshod over everyone.

I believe Eights think they are protecting themselves by being in charge. However, being the one who always leads, controls, and makes decisions in a relationship can be isolating. And it often keeps Eights from learning to handle the surprises that life inevitably brings. It's important to note that we all protect ourselves from certain things (for example, Nines protect themselves from conflict, Sevens are very conscientious about avoiding pain, and Fours are diligent in their concern about abandonment). Eights are committed to protecting themselves from unexpected emotions, but as you can see with Nadia's story, Eights need to learn to not run roughshod over everyone.

THE PATH TOGETHER

Eights are demonstrably clear about how they relate to others. If you watch them, it's obvious who does and who does not have access to their softer, more tender side. My daughter Joey and I were teaching together one day when she offered the group a very clear statement of how an Eight approaches relationships at work.

Cupping her hands, she explained, "I only have this much 'warm and fuzzy' in me. That is absolutely it. There is no more. Ever. Most of that goes to my husband and my sons. Whatever I have left over goes to making authentic personal connections with prospective clients. I do not inquire about my colleagues' personal lives, and I don't share details about mine. I come to work every day to do the job that I have been tasked to do—and I place great importance on doing that job well. If my colleagues can put their energy into doing their job well, we can enjoy the camaraderie of that effort together. If not, I have nothing to share with them. I have friends. I do not come to work to explore friendships."

Though it will be counterintuitive, it is vital for Eights to realize that bringing your feelings into balance as you encounter others will be beneficial to you and to those in relationship with you. Because your feelings have not made a regular appearance in your arsenal for taking on the world, they are one of the purest parts of your being. Allowing yourself to stop and consider how you feel about a situation and taking those feelings into consideration before *doing* will serve you well as you make your way on this fantastic Enneagram journey.

RELATIONSHIPS *for* EIGHTS

After all is said and done . . .

One of the greatest gifts of the Enneagram is that it teaches us what we can have, what we can't have, and what we just have to accept and allow. For Eights, everyone else can't be as strong as you are. Here are some other things for Eights to keep in mind:

You can . . .

- be in leadership positions if you have people who are willing to follow you—and that requires respecting how they see the world.
- realize that you can lead and make plans, although you can't control the outcomes.
- hire people who are aggressive, but remember you will always have to work with people who are not.
- learn the value of moderation, collaboration, and patience—and cultivate the self-awareness to practice them.
- protect yourself emotionally, remembering that you can't avoid vulnerability.

But you can't . . .

- be fully heard without giving consideration to the other eight ways of receiving information.
- avoid or deny vulnerability and still be successful in relationships.
- always lead—you must learn to follow another leader gracefully.
- affect the world without being affected by it.
- solve every problem with action and strength.
- share feelings you haven't allowed yourself to experience.

So you'll need to accept that . . .

- you're not always right.
- you can't guarantee the outcome.
- you thrive on stress, but other people don't.
- there's something bigger than yourself to focus on.

The main thing to keep in mind in relationship with Eights is that their aggression is not personal. They mean no harm, so don't be misled by their strong opinions and passions. Here are some additional ways you can build better relationships with the Eights in your life:

- Even though Eights are strong and assertive, don't forget that they still need care.

- If you don't stand up for yourself, if you are not forthcoming, if you fail to be honest, and if you are indirect, then you are invisible to Eights.

- Don't beat around the bush: Eights want communication to be brief, straightforward, and truthful.

- Be aware that Eights are controlling in relationships simply because they don't want to be controlled.

- Bring your best effort to anything you do. Do what you say you will do and let them know you are all in—or not.

- Eights don't like it when you talk behind their back—and they don't understand why you would. Given the opportunity, they would say to you, "Why would you tell somebody else what you think about me? Tell *me*. I can handle it."

- If Eights are not happy with you, they tell you. If they don't tell you but seem a little distant, it most likely has nothing to do with you.

- Acknowledge the contributions that Eights make, but don't flatter them because they neither trust nor need flattery.

- Encourage Eights to exercise regularly. A good exercise program uses up some of their excess energy.

- Be aware that Eights sometimes mistake tenderness for manipulation.

- Intensity is always well-received. Be secure and strong in yourself and in what you think and believe.

- Keep in mind that Eights are often unaware of how they affect others.

9s

RISKING CONFLICT FOR CONNECTION

*A*ndy Gullahorn, a Nine who happens to be a very talented musician, has a remarkable story about his first big gig as a high school kid in Austin, Texas.

The greatest things in my career happened when I was sixteen or seventeen years old. I started playing guitar in high school, and I learned quickly because I'd been playing piano for a long time. The guitar easily became my preference. A woman who worked with my dad at his law firm also had a country cover band, and she asked if I wanted to play rhythm guitar for some event outside of Austin. I wanted to play with almost anybody, almost anywhere, so of course I said yes.

The gig was in a fire hall in Pedernales, Texas. I was having fun playing with the band and people were singing along and dancing in the driveway. We played

four or five songs and everyone was having a great time
when I looked up and Willie Nelson was walking toward
us. It was his birthday and the Pedernales Fire Hall is
adjacent to his farm. He knew the lady who was singing,
and after they talked for a bit she said, "Well, do you
want to play some songs?"

Willie said, "Yeah, sure." He came up and we played
for a couple of hours. I was happy to be on rhythm guitar,
playing harmony in whatever key Willie chose. I knew
all of his songs so it was no problem for me. We all really
enjoyed ourselves and making music together. At one
point I did think, this is my first real gig and I'm playing
backup with Willie Nelson!

We never actually met but when we were done I said,
"Thanks," and he said, "Thank you," and that was it.

What's Going on Here?

How do you imagine yourself in this situation, from beginning to end?

How do you think your response to the night, playing rhythm guitar with
Willie, would differ from Andy's?

How does the Enneagram explain the difference between Andy's response
and what you think yours would be?

If you're a sixteen-year-old musician in Texas and your first
gig turns into a night of playing rhythm guitar for Willie
Nelson, it's a very big deal. Unless, of course, you're like Andy:
a Nine who can emotionally detach from the experience of

playing backup for a country music legend. The truth is that we need to know ourselves based on how we relate to strangers in order to better understand how we relate to people we are with from day-to-day. Nines have the ability to disconnect in any relationship.

Nines have a tendency to erase themselves from events. Being relational with someone, no matter who it is or for how long, is an experience of vulnerability that differs for all of us. Nines manage that exposure by assuring themselves that their presence doesn't matter. They can contribute what they have to offer, or not, believing that it won't affect the outcome either way. But Willie Nelson had a great birthday celebration at the Pedernales Fire Hall in part because he got to play his guitar and sing the songs he loves. And the music was better that night for Willie and for everyone else because Andy Gullahorn already knew all of Willie's songs and could play rhythm guitar in any key. Andy's presence was not inconsequential for anybody but Andy.

When Nines are able to entertain the idea that their presence matters, it has a positive effect on all of their encounters with others, especially those they love the most.

THE WORLD OF NINES

Nines have the least energy of all the numbers on the Enneagram. They are easygoing and undemanding—they just don't rock the boat—because in their experience, intensity and desires often result in discomfort and trouble. But it takes a lot of energy to maintain that easygoing approach all day.

My husband, Joe, is a Nine. Even though he is the best person I know, he is easily distracted. My schedule is so full that it's rare for me to be home on a weekend that is not a holiday. Years ago, on such a weekend, Joe shared that he was so excited to have me home that he made plans for spending those days with one intention in mind: spoiling me. The plan included sleeping in, breakfast in bed, movies, naps—and time with him, which, for me, is the greatest treasure of all.

Saturday morning when we woke, he suggested that I stay in bed and read and promised that he would return with my coffee. I chose one of the books from my nightstand and began to read. I read . . . and read . . . and read. Finally, I heard the front door open. Then I heard the pantry door open and close. I took note when I heard the newspaper hitting the kitchen counter and the beep from the alarm system on the door to the garage. I was beginning to wonder if he even remembered that I was in the house when I heard the familiar squeaking of our garage door opening, followed by the sound of our lawn mower.

> You can't change how you see—you can only change what you *do* with how you see.

Standing on the back patio, hands on my hips with an expression that Joe describes as equal parts curiosity and disappointment, I felt forgotten, unimportant, and overlooked.

Seeing me, Joe dropped the handle to the lawnmower and insisted that I get back in bed, saying he would be there immediately with my coffee. Moments later there he was, standing in the doorway holding my coffee mug and saying, "Do you even want to know what happened?"

"I'm dying to know what happened!"

"Well, I was headed to the kitchen when I heard the neighbor's cat at the front door. When I went to shoo away the cat, the newspaper was there so I picked it up, took it out of the plastic sack, and threw the sack in the trash. I put the newspaper on the counter and the ad pages were right on top. Guess what? Home Depot has weed eater twine on sale! I know you don't know much about weed eater twine but . . ."

"You've got me there, I don't actually know anything about our weed eater and its twine."

"Well, it's expensive and it comes in several sizes. I went to the garage to see what size we use and the good news is ours is the one on sale and it's buy one, get one free. How great is that! So, I put the weed eater back on the hook next to the lawn mower and I thought, it's a beautiful morning. I should mow!"

If you're in a relationship with a Nine, you will have to accept that their lives are made up of distractions. Even when intentional about their focus, they often get lost in doing something that isn't part of the plan for the day. When they get distracted from you, don't take it personally because it isn't about you—it's all about *how they see*. Nines follow whatever passes in front of them, regardless of the task at hand. They frequently tell me that they are constantly addressing their propensity for distraction.

CONFLICT AND SELF-PROTECTION. Everyone avoids something, and Nines avoid conflict. From their perspective, very few things are worth arguing about unless a decision involves their integrity. They certainly don't want to waste time arguing over what they call "the little stuff"—perhaps that is the secret to their peacefulness.

People are drawn to Nines and want to get to know them. But sometimes it feels to the Nine like other people want too much from them—they want to know all about them, who they are and what they stand for. That can be a real challenge because Nines tend to merge with the ideas and agendas of others in order to avoid conflict. And when they do, it often leaves others feeling somewhat confused, wondering if the Nine can be trusted.

Dr. Chris Gonzalez, a marriage and family therapist, explains this phenomenon of Nines merging with others:

> I have struggled to find or understand myself because I tend to change the expression of my personality dramatically and radically depending on who I'm with and where we are. If I'm with someone who is emotionally very expressive, I tend to be very emotional. If the people around me have dominant personalities or are driven to

unhealthy conflict or anger, I choose to be submissive. I will likely do whatever it takes to appease their anger and maximize peace.

Although the motivation for this action is to maintain his sense of peace, Chris understands how confusing and unhealthy this behavior can be for ongoing relationships with people who are present in his everyday life.

Nines probably don't ever really embrace conflict, but they can learn to lean into difficult conversations by courageously saying what they think and naming their preferences without losing anything. When they do, it's almost always good for their relationships. When they don't, the other person is left to guess, suppose, and hope. Mike McHargue (AKA "Science Mike," who hosts *The Liturgist Podcast*) explains how conflict can help grow relationships:

> When I understand that I am averse to even healthy conflict, and healthy conflict actually produces intimacy, and it strengthens relationships, that insight lets me take intentional steps toward exploring and experiencing conflict when necessary to mitigate some of the weaker or more difficult aspects of my personality. That's an insight I never would have found without the Enneagram.

Guessing, supposing, and hoping in a relationship is exhausting, unhealthy, and for the most part unproductive. Like anyone else, Nines have desires and ideas and preferences.

And they are perfectly capable of naming them if they are willing to risk it. Moreover, their relationships are better for it.

SLOTH. Nines are often misunderstood, but in the gentle sort of way. They are always working but sometimes they're working on the right thing at the wrong time. A Nine recently told me about hearing a pastor in Abilene, Texas, redefine sloth: "It's not lazy—it's getting busy doing something that keeps you from doing what you ought to be doing." After thinking about sloth in these new terms, it hit him hard. "I am very, very good at doing things and convincing everyone that what I'm doing is important to do. But the truth is, I'm energized by my neglect of that other thing that I should be doing but don't want to do." Such valuable insight that only a Nine would be able to explain!

Nines get energy from avoiding what needs to be done. In fact, some of their best thoughts or most creative thinking happens while they are avoiding the tasks that, for one reason or another, require their immediate attention. However, those in relationship with Nines seldom understand this dynamic, believing the Nine is lazy and assuming that if things are going to be handled, they will have to do it themselves.

RIGHT ACTION. One of the most appreciable aspects of the Enneagram is that it offers a safety net for every personality type. The counterpart to Nines merging for the sake of peace in matters that seem inconsequential is called *right action*, and it is essential for understanding relationships. When a decision to act includes potential for conflict and negative consequences, yet the action is chosen anyway, this is considered *right* action. Nines are *not* wishy-washy, malleable people who have no boundaries. But they *are* people who have a limited amount of energy, and they are mindful about how they use it. There are many things that other numbers take very seriously that Nines just can't get worked up about. For them, most things aren't worth the risk and loss that are part and parcel of conflict. But when something is really important—when it involves a decision that is consequential for a lifetime—Nines are forthcoming, courageous, committed, and determined. Science Mike explains it this way: "I've learned how to say what I believe and say it confidently and that has created a trajectory in my life that looks like I'm trying to achieve, but what's actually happening is I've found a methodology that makes my peacemaking efforts successful."

Disagreement about where to go on vacation or even to dinner can be unnerving for a Nine. But when they know, without a doubt, that they need to make choices that address important and extremely conflictual situations, they proceed without hesitation. There is a certain sense

> Sometimes Nines appear distracted or disengaged, but that does not necessarily indicate a lack of interest.
>
> 9

of self-worth and value that comes from standing up for something that is so important it cannot be compromised for what would end up being pseudopeace. It may not happen often, but when it does, Nines and their relationships are changed for the better.

ANGER. Like Eights and Ones, Nines are in the Anger Triad at the top of the Enneagram. You know when Eights are angry with you—they are clear about why and they wait for your response, then go on with their day. Not so with passive-aggressive Nines. They're quietly stubborn—perhaps the most stubborn number on the Enneagram. They refuse to be nagged or pushed or coerced into doing anything, so if that's your method in relating to a Nine you will experience a lot of frustration and disappointment with very little success. Nines have their ways of letting you know they are hurt or angry, but none of them are direct. You can avoid getting hooked by the Nine's vague suggestions and non-verbal demonstrations of hurt or dissatisfaction, but it will take some time, energy, and understanding from both of you.

In Enneagram wisdom, the best part of you is also the worst part of you.

Since they aren't good tacticians when they feel angry, Nines buy time with passive expressions of their feelings. They are concerned that direct and aggressive verbal exchanges will result in fragmentation. But they also worry about being able to contain their own anger once they give it a voice and full rein.

If you engage Nines in a difficult conversation because *you* are angry, they will usually just sit it out until you've stopped talking. Then they will methodically avoid both you and the subject until things settle. Regardless of where the anger originates, they will likely choose to go away, making themselves unavailable and believing that with time the problem will fix itself. Nines have to learn that taking leave in situations like this usually increases frustration and anger, leaving things far from "fixed."

If you're in a relationship with a Nine, please keep in mind that when they are passive-aggressive they are also communicating their hurt and disappointment—just not directly. My husband, Joe, for example, will normally call me at my home office about an hour and a half after he leaves for work at his church. When things are not quite right in our relationship, he doesn't call until late morning. When I ask if something is

9s and Others

1s: When Ones have thought things through and are ready to move forward, Nines often want to stay on the fence. Nines need to remember that although there is wisdom in waiting for a time, there is also a time for action.

2s: Relationships between Twos and Nines are common and are usually successful. Nines can contribute to relationships by teaching Twos that responding to every feeling they pick up from others is neither necessary nor healthy. Nines can also help Twos recognize their tendency to overreach into the lives of others.

3s & 6s: Nines share a line with both Threes and Sixes on the Enneagram, moving to Six in stress and Three in security. Nines need the confidence of a Three to know they have something valuable to offer and that their full participation in life is welcomed by others. Sixes offer Nines an awareness of appropriate times to accept that not everyone can be trusted; the desire to be unaffected by life will be significantly challenged for Nines who refuse to acknowledge this.

4s: In a long-term relationship with a Four, a Nine's lack of intensity can become a problem.

5s: Nines will have to ask for what they want and need in a relationship with a Five. If Nines can commit to that, it will be good for both.

7s: Nines and Sevens share a wonderful view of the world. Both are open-minded and share an appreciation for diversity. But Nines will have to be careful about going along to avoid fragmentation. Sevens need Nines to be mindful about consequences because that is not Sevens' strong suit.

8s: Nines can't allow Eights to define their relationship. It isn't fair and it shows a lack of respect for both of you. But Eights and Nines can actually be a really great combination if Nines show up and are real.

9s: When Nines are in relationship with other Nines, they should each lead the way in questioning the status quo.

wrong, he usually denies it and then insists that he has to hang up and will call back later. What's really happening here is that Joe is either hurt by something I have done or failed to do, or he is angry. He wants me to know that, but he doesn't want to discuss it. His preference would be that I acknowledge that he is unhappy, figure out why, avoid doing what caused his displeasure in the future, and go on with life as if nothing happened.

In all fairness I must say that after working at it for years, Joe is much better about communicating directly. And our relationship is better because of his effort. I don't know that we would have been able to name this habitual response to hurt and disappointment, choosing to work toward something different, if we hadn't known the Enneagram.

STRESS AND SECURITY

Nines in stress are often withdrawn, indecisive, noncommunicative, secretive, and stubborn. They are usually absent (emotionally and physically), and if they are present, they're either unable or unwilling to risk connecting with others. Nines don't want to be controlled or affected by anything, which causes them to diminish the importance of dealing with perceived obstacles. But Nines living in this pattern of behavior run the risk of missing opportunities they never get back. When it comes to relationships, life happens in real time, and you have to be truly present to experience it.

When Nines in stress take on the mature and healthier behavior of a Six, they are often able to affect their environment in meaningful ways. With some Six onboard, a Nine is usually more outspoken, especially as it relates to what would be best for the common good. Our daughter Jenny, a Nine and an administrator in a Catholic school system, became a voice for the entire faculty when the pay scale in their system was changed in ways that didn't honor the teachers who had been teaching in the school for years. Both her voice and her involvement were a surprise to everyone. Nines are very concerned about justice issues, so it should not be surprising when stressed Nines speak up and move into action in an effort to make things right.

> Some Enneagram numbers prefer predictability while others require spontaneity.

When life is running smoothly and Nines are feeling secure, they are able to take advantage of some behavior patterns that are usually associated with Threes. Essentially, that means they are all about performing and doing and accomplishing. In this space, Nines set goals for themselves that are attainable. Partners and coworkers are especially pleased when Nines step up, sure of themselves, and confident in doing their part.

LIMITATIONS IN RELATIONSHIPS

It is harder for a Nine to know who they are in a relationship than for any other number. They seem to arrive on the planet with a desire to be unaffected by life and with a propensity toward merging with the ideas and agendas of others. Chris Gonzalez explains it better than anyone I've ever heard. He says that in a significant conversation with others, he starts to "blend into what they're saying" to him or about him. He says that "it's like looking into a foggy mirror—I can't really see or hear myself because I'm trying to see someone else."

Chris's response provides a key insight:

> When I am sharing space with someone who has good boundaries, I automatically merge with them. It would take too much energy to separate what I think and feel from what the other person expresses with such clarity. But when the other person is gone, I can think more clearly and know what I want, what I think, and what I believe. It requires a lot of energy for me to know myself. So, if I'm using up that energy to know you, then I have a weird amnesia about me.

In relationships with Nines, we often appreciate their merging with our agendas because it means we get to have things our way. Then it becomes both surprising and problematic when suddenly they pop up with a strong opinion or desire that is in conflict with what we want. Even so, it is far better for relationships when Nines establish some consistency in verbalizing what they think, want, and need.

Communication with a Nine can be confusing. It should be no surprise that Nines will often just say what you want them to say or choose to say nothing—they see it as protecting their relationship with you. Until they've done some personal work, they have no idea that instead of preservation, they introduce fragmentation when they are not able or not willing to be honest.

In thinking about Nines, their merging and how they inhabit the world, it would be easy to fall into believing that they are prone to yield to peer pressure. They are not. Merging from the Nine's perspective is for matters of little consequence. Nines accurately see themselves as capable of making their own decisions and acting on them with or without the support of others. They are, in fact, independent. They think independently and they are content to act alone. Acutely aware of what others want from

Nines do best when they have someone to help hold them accountable for their goals.

9

them, Nines won't risk their own integrity in order to join in an activity or belong to a group. However, unlike most other numbers, Nines are quiet about their disapproval; they have no desire for anyone to notice their lack of participation.

When I was in my teens a very long time ago, the language we used when we wanted permission for something our parents seemed opposed to was "Everyone is doing it." And parents responded with something like, "If everyone jumped off the bridge, would you jump off too?" Nines won't jump off the bridge, but they will let you jump if you want to.

In relation to choices and behavior, Nines are the least controlling of all the numbers. Their appreciation for independence is a two-way street: they want theirs and they want you to have yours.

THE PATH TOGETHER

I frequently tell others about my friend Patsy, who teaches visually impaired children. One fall at the parent-student orientation meeting, an ophthalmologist brought a pair of glasses for each parent to try on that replicates what their children can and cannot see.

The result was astonishing. "Parents were hugging their children and telling them how proud they were, and the children were basking in praise they so desperately longed for," tells Patsy. The special glasses revealed to parents the challenges for their children. "Parental expectations were replaced with disbelief when they realized all that their children were able to accomplish while able to see so little."

This story has had a significant effect on Bill Millican, who lost his vision to a congenital disease at thirty-seven. "Patsy gave us a real-world example of how people see the world differently, and how important it is to do what we can to see the world as others see it."

In his professional life, Bill is a mediator. He told me that because he is a Nine, he can almost always see and empathize with all sides of a conflict. He says, "It remains clear to me that a good mediator or peacemaker is one that can see, understand, and empathize with every side of life. This doesn't mean that I don't have strong feelings about one side or another in a conflict. It just means that I can clearly articulate the view of everyone in the discussion. In the end, isn't that what everyone is looking for? A chance to be understood as they talk about life as they see it."

Unfortunately, our judgment about others is formed without the benefit of being able to see as they see. Like the parents of these children, we are blind to the obstacles that determine how others live their lives and navigate the world. Relationships are surely compromised by this lack of vision.

Nines see two sides to everything, for better and for worse. This makes it very difficult for Nines to make a decision, which leads to merging in relationships. However, when healthy Nines are willing to articulate what they want, they are usually on the right track, headed in the right direction, for the right reasons. When this happens, everybody benefits.

RELATIONSHIPS *for* NINES

After all is said and done ...

Understanding what we can and can't control is part of the Enneagram journey.
Nines need to remember that their voice matters because they matter. Here are a few
other things for Nines to keep in mind:

You can ...

- learn really good tools for avoiding some conflicts and resolving others.
- learn to manage the tension between regretting being compliant and being
  afraid of being noncompliant.
- recognize that relationships are best when you do not give up your personal
  identity.
- take steps to engage conflict in a healthy way, understanding that avoiding
  conflict often causes conflict.

But you can't ...

- always avoid conflict.
- ignore the reality that "later" is not a point in time.
- avoid fragmentation and loss in relationships. Some relationships don't
  last—and perhaps they weren't intended to.
- expect people to read your mind.
- be healthy and whole if you spend your life setting yourself aside in order to
  stay connected to others.

So you'll need to accept that ...

- problems don't fix themselves.
- there are times when you must assert yourself. It is yours to do, regardless
  of the cost.
- there is no such thing as a healthy relationship that is void of anger,
  disappointment, and conflict.
- your presence in the lives of those around you matters a lot. They rely on you,
  they trust you, and they want your full involvement in the life you share.

Nines need lots of affirmation and affection, so if a Nine has the strength to say an honest "no" to you, let them know how much you appreciate their honesty and that you aren't going away, regardless of their response. Here are some other things to keep in mind in relationships with Nines:

- Nines have their own desires and dreams and preferences—encourage them to name them.
- Encourage Nines to develop their own identity in relationship with you.
- Nines appreciate, and perhaps need, a peaceful environment.
- Nines both want and need alone time, their own space, and independence.
- Avoid saying, "Don't you think we should _____?" The answer will almost always be yes, and it will often not be what the Nine thinks or wants. Instead, try asking, "Do you think we should _____?"
- Focus on what Nines *do* as opposed to what they forget or fail to do.
- Don't interrupt when Nines are talking. Make room for them to meander a bit—they will get to the point.
- Remember that Nines have a generous spirit. If you aren't mindful, it is easy to take advantage of them.
- Nines don't like confrontation, but that doesn't mean you should never confront them. Opposing points of view are part of life.
- Encourage Nines to share their grievances with you.
- Nines want clear, direct communication regarding what's expected of them.
- When a Nine is distracted by nonessentials, you can redirect their energy by asking questions.
- Remember this: agreement doesn't always lead to participation, and when Nines do participate it doesn't necessarily indicate commitment.
- Nines don't make personal decisions quickly, and they don't usually want your help.

1s

THINGS COULD
ALWAYS BE BETTER

*O*ne sultry summer afternoon when I was teaching an introductory Enneagram conference in Nashville, I noticed a handsome young couple sitting near the front. Amanda was well-dressed, attentive, and looked like a very kind person. Christopher was equally well put together: neatly pressed shirt, neatly trimmed beard, and an expression of careful attention. They listened intently as I started teaching about Eights and Nines, taking notes and at times nodding in agreement and recognition. But when I started talking about Ones, everything changed. They seemed uncomfortable and surprised. They kept looking at each other or leaning forward as if to hear me better, and the more I talked, the more distressed they seemed. Amanda was crying off and on, and Christopher attempted to comfort her while obviously struggling to manage his own feelings.

It was then that I suspected they were both Ones.

When Ones hear their number taught, it's both a relief and a surprise. They often nod in agreement when I describe how they see. They sit up a little straighter when they hear about their gifts for assessing every situation and seeing potential for improvement. And I really get their attention when I talk about the inner critic that constantly reminds them that they could both *do* better and *be* better.

Amanda says, "The main thing about a One is that nothing is ever good enough. I constantly strive for perfection, yet there is no way to achieve it. It's impossible." Christopher agrees: "Good enough is good enough for everybody else, but I've got to be right. And not just *kind of* right. I don't want to make a C, I want to make an A+."

What's Going on Here?

What do you think it would be like to have a relentless inner critical voice constantly telling you that nothing is good enough?

How could that voice and its demands for perfection affect your relationships?

What is the difference, in your opinion, between being good and being right?

When it comes to relationships, it's really important to remember that you can't change how you see—you can only change what you do with how you see. Unlike Ones, some numbers don't notice what's out of place or not working, and others may notice but not care. With all of this in mind, you can see how *perfection* is a word often associated with Ones. But they don't like it.

When Ian Cron and I wrote *The Road Back to You*, we had several conversations about how we would name Ones. The Ones I know suggested the "Reformer" or the "Evaluator," and we considered both of those along with other suggestions we received. The truth is that most Ones spend much of their lives seeking perfection in thought and word and deed. They do so for honorable reasons, but that doesn't change the fact that they do it. And perfection is like an ice sculpture: it lasts only as long as there's no change in the atmosphere.

> The Enneagram teaches us that the nine ways we deal with crisis are both habitual and predictable.

If you're in a relationship with Ones, know that you will have to contend with a critic that you can't hear, but that finds fault with most of what Ones do and think, and tells them they are flawed in some terrible, unredeemable way. Unfortunately, their method of coping is to find fault in others—often finding fault in *you*. They believe criticism is caring, so they have to be taught that not everybody feels the same way about being corrected or encouraged to seek improvement.

For Ones like Amanda and Christopher, their relationship is beautiful and complicated: they share a desire for perfection, but they have different priorities about what needs to be perfected. For this couple, their individual critical voices will be a force they will have to deal with for their entire lives. They are managing, but their challenge is to learn to accept a certain amount of imperfection in themselves and in others, and then find a way to be comfortable with it.

A One's first response to everything is "How can I make this better?" That's good as long as they recognize that other people may be thinking, "How can I finish this and move on?" or, "Do I really need to finish this or can I live with what I've already done?" or, "Surely this is good enough" or even, "So what if it is missing one little part—let them do it if they want to keep tweaking it." It's difficult for Ones to understand, much less respect, people who don't want to give their best to every endeavor. They struggle to accept anything less. And if they try to, it tends to make them miserable.

One of my long-time students told me a story that illustrates this desire for perfection. He started by telling me that I had ruined his life. Since I'm accustomed to having people tell me that I've saved their lives or that the Enneagram has saved their lives, I wasn't sure how to respond.

"How did I ruin your life?"

"Well, as you probably know, I'm in seminary now so we needed some extra space for books. We bought one of those bookcases that requires an Allen wrench, some assembly, a sense of humor, and lots of patience. The instructions included a diagram of all the parts, and the prompt that if anything was missing, I should call the 1-800 number at the bottom of the page. It guaranteed that I would receive my order within ten working days.

"When I found that I was indeed missing two nails, one screw, and a decorative screw cover, I thought I'd better order them and do this right. Then I heard your voice in my head, saying, in that way you say things, 'Who does that?!' In the weakness of that moment I agreed with you. Ignoring the other voice in my head and abandoning my better judgment, I put the bookcase together without the missing parts."

I congratulated him on accommodating these small imperfections, but it was soon abundantly clear that he was neither proud of the choice he made nor thankful for my influence. He said, "I can't stand to be in the same room with that damn bookcase! Every time I look at it, I think of those missing pieces and my irresponsibility in putting it together the *lazy* way. It finally became such a distraction we had to move it to the back of the house where I seldom see it. Every time I think about that bookcase I'm disappointed in myself!"

The problem comes when different Enneagram types try to agree on what to do.

There isn't another number on the Enneagram that demands so much and rewards so sparingly. Imperfection is everywhere, and even if some semblance of perfection is achieved, it lasts about as long as a snowflake in the noonday sun. It's a struggle for most of us to imagine the exhaustion of living with an inner voice criticizing us and our choices all day, every day. But if we're trying to figure out life with Ones and we ignore these realities, there is little chance that our relationships will be satisfying.

ANGER. Just about every summer, my mother, like most other women in the farming and ranching community of Texas where I grew up, canned and preserved the abundant fresh summer vegetables and fruits. She and the neighbors spent a day or more every week canning corn, green beans, and tomatoes in huge pressure cookers that were heavy and complicated and somewhat of a mystery to me. The steam in the cooker was measured by a regulator that sat on top, rocking when the pressure was right and blowing when it was too much.

This image of steam building up in a pressure cooker is a good way to describe what happens with anger in Ones. Sometimes Ones seethe with anger. This is hard on their relationships and causes deep regret, so it's very important that Ones, and those they love, get whatever help is necessary to manage their anger.

> **1** After finishing a project, Ones often focus on what could have been done better instead of celebrating its completion.

Keep in mind that anger in Ones doesn't usually manifest as blowing up and yelling, but as something a bit more insidious: *resentment*. When Ones are angry at something, they turn that anger in on themselves first and it feels like shame—shame about the faults and failings of themselves and others. Shame adds a bitter quality that results in a complex resentment, something others need to understand in relationship with Ones.

Jenay is a wife, a mom of three teenage boys, and a high school administrator. She's your typical One: organized, detail oriented, hard working, and the kind of friend who wouldn't hesitate to pick you up from the airport at 2 a.m. But she admits to being derailed by her Oneness more than a time or two.

Such an event occurred on a family vacation with two little kids and another on the way. "We were staying with family in Phoenix and decided to take a day trip to Sedona," Jenay recounts. "I had planned on getting some great photos of the boys—especially something we could use for our Christmas card."

Unfortunately, only a few miles from their destination, Jenay realized that the camera was not in the car. "Honestly, at first I wanted to blame my husband. But I had to get over that pretty quickly since he *never* takes pictures—the camera is mine, and I just flat forgot to bring it." This was pre–cell phones, so Jenay's husband stopped at a Walgreens and walked out with a disposable camera. "Every scene in Sedona was so picturesque, and there I was taking pictures with a disposable camera. *A disposable camera!*"

Jenay admits to being "an all-around grouch—barely speaking" as they hiked around and explored the beautiful red rocks. By lunchtime she had cooled off, but was obviously still distracted by the error of her ways. "It was then that my husband, lovingly but firmly, looked me in the eyes and said, 'You need to let this go—you can't let a stupid camera ruin our whole day.'"

Ones frequently miss the bigger picture because they compulsively focus on what is wrong or out of place. "We had two adorable little boys who were giddy about the adventure of exploring, and I was a mess," admits Jenay. "I just couldn't stop kicking myself that I forgot the camera. Even though I've learned how to not be so consumed by my self-loathing in the years since, the memory of the forgotten camera is still much more vivid than anything else from that day."

It's important to know that Ones are often frustrated yet are seldom angered by what they appear to be angry about. Jenay was frustrated by the forgotten camera, not because she wasn't able to capture the events of the day on film but because forgetting the camera meant that she had failed. When Ones feel anger, they deny it, stuff it, rename it, move on—and then they manage it by perfecting something that is within their control, like making sure to remember every little thing (checklists!) for the next outing.

Ones love deeply and well. They do all they can to protect and care for those they are in relationship with. They are thoughtful, careful, mindful, and supportive. But it's hard to get things right with a One, even in a relationship. Try to remember that their responses have everything to do with how they see, and, through no fault of their own, they see imperfection everywhere. Keep in mind that Ones are also much harder on themselves than they are on anyone else, and that they deeply regret it when their patience is limited and their expectations are unreasonable—especially at home.

DISCONNECTION FROM THINKING. Ones tend to see life in terms of responsibility and work. They are focused on whatever is happening right in front of them and then try to respond appropriately by doing whatever the situation requires. Ones feel deeply about what they do and how well they respond in each situation. Oftentimes this limits the energy they have left for the emotional needs and expectations within their relationships.

Thankfully, there's a solution. But Ones tend to push back when I point out that they often leave out thinking when deciding what is theirs to do and how they should do it. They believe they're thinking all the time. The truth is that an ongoing internal dialogue with that pesky critic is not the same thing as thinking. In fact, often what Ones mistake for thinking is merely responding to their inner critic's prompts. Mary, an Episcopal priest, wife, and mother of two sons, explains it this way:

> Ones are usually the first to respond to a need.

Ones always know something else needs to be done, so we don't give ourselves any space to relax. And what that does unintentionally in relationships is it doesn't allow the other people around us to relax either. So, if I'm in the house, whether I'm saying anything or not, and I'm all jittery because I know I still have a couple of things on my to-do list, I can't be still. There is no reason why those things couldn't be done tomorrow. They don't have to be done today, but I'm thinking, "I have a little block of time and I should get that thing done." When I respond to that urge to keep doing, I send a message to everyone in my household that they can't relax either. "If I'm working you guys need to be working. If I'm not calm you guys can't be calm either."

If Ones can balance doing with awareness of feelings and some thoughtful discernment, they might make different choices. And choosing differently can add to the goodness and health of their relationships.

FEAR OF BEING BAD. I have lots of Ones in my life and I really like them. They are charming, interesting, and engaging. Even though Ones appear to be secure and fairly sure of themselves, we know that everyone is fearful about something; Ones are afraid of being bad. Because Ones came to believe that meeting the expectations of others would, in some way, make them more valuable and offer them some much-desired security, relationships became more about performing well than relating well and loving well.

But the more Ones focus on what other people want from them, the more they lose touch with their own needs and desires. Once this pattern is set in motion, they only understand their own goodness by how well they measure up to what others define as good. After a time, rules, standards, and directives become the boundaries that determine how Ones evaluate the success or failure of their day. Unfortunately, Ones often tell me that they can't live up to the standards they set for themselves, and the potential for making everything better seems to follow them like a shadow.

My heart is full of respect and tenderness for Ones. When they wear this mantle of fear and expectation into adulthood, life can be very demanding. In a relationship with a One, honesty is essential, but telling them that they are good in ways that they can hear it is the greater gift. Do it as often as you can in all the ways you can.

STRESS AND SECURITY

On their best days, when Ones are healthy in their relationships, they are relaxed and charming and fun. Ones are always conscientious, so they will do a good job at whatever is important to them. And when they're at their best, Ones can make room for a difference in opinion as to what constitutes a "good job."

When Ones are in low average space, they are argumentative and uncompromising. They have many expectations, and when expectations aren't met, resentment soon follows. They are picky and unpredictable, and your efforts to please them often fail. These behaviors represent excess in Oneness, which is never a good thing. We all struggle when we are on the low side of average behavior for our number. So, to honor our relationships, we all need to watch for behavior that exaggerates the things that seem important from our point of view but end up causing separation between us and the people we care about.

When Ones are experiencing too much stress, they begin to assign moral value to mistakes. If others miss a deadline or forget a meeting, it can escalate. Ones might first label the coworker as lazy or indifferent, but that can deteriorate to labels like useless or no good. Labels like that can wound and damage or even change a relationship permanently. Keep in mind that such behavior comes directly from the way Ones berate themselves when they make a mistake or miss a deadline, so they do the same to others. But other numbers don't abuse themselves in that way, so they struggle to tolerate such behavior.

The natural response for Ones in stressful times is to focus on what they can perfect. I have a good friend who is a One who says, "When the world is going to hell, I clean my bathroom."

Thankfully, the Enneagram shows us the intuitive moves toward other numbers that can save us pain and suffering while helping to protect our relationships. In times of stress,

Ones move to Four, where they can get in touch with a different way of experiencing and expressing their feelings. With Four energy, they don't have to accept the notion that they are bad or corrupt or lazy or stupid (a few of the labels Ones reserve for themselves). Instead, they can get in touch with some feelings that don't need fixing. This is good—the critic cannot be as loud about feelings as it is about actions, so the One will get a reprieve. Then they can regroup and reconnect with the world in a much healthier way.

When Ones are feeling secure they have access to Seven energy and behavior, and that allows them to relax a little. They can look at life and work and relationships with less judgment and more acceptance and peace. And they can allow themselves to have some fun.

My dad was a One and my mom a Five. By the time they adopted me, they must have worked through and

1s and Others

1s: Ones in relationship with other Ones will experience understanding. However, perpetual dissatisfaction opens the door to using improvement as the measure in most aspects of the relationship. Truly, some things are good enough as they are.

2s: Ones and Twos respond to life differently. Ones are practical while Twos are relational. Ones tend to think that Twos can't stay focused, while Twos think Ones are too rigid, but both need to cultivate the art of compromise.

3s: Ones and Threes both want to get things done, and both want to be the best. But Threes cut corners, while Ones believe every step of a task should be done correctly. Ones need to be careful about judging different paths toward the same goal.

4s: The emotional needs of Ones are often repressed, so Ones can learn from Fours how to focus on feelings rather than falling into the pattern of dualistic thinking. And Fours can benefit from the ability of Ones to stay focused and see things through to the end. This relationship can be extremely advantageous for both.

5s: In relating to a Five, Ones will need to let go of the notion that silence represents judgment. Fives are silent much of the time, and they are rarely, if ever, judging. Ones need to avoid making assumptions about what others are thinking.

6s: Along with Twos and Sixes, Ones respond to whatever is happening right in front of them, in part because the initial reaction is to *do* something. Ones need to keep in mind that their way isn't the only right way.

7s: Sevens need the discipline of Ones, and Ones need the flexibility and spontaneity of Sevens. With some awareness they can be a great team.

8s: Ones and Eights are both dualistic, right/wrong thinkers, both think they're right most of the time, and both have a tendency at times to react without thinking things through. On the more positive side, Ones appreciate that Eights are so free while Eights admire the discipline of Ones.

9s: Ones have a lot in common with Nines: both repress anger, though for different reasons. They both also like to ruminate about decisions for a long time, so be aware that someone will have to step up when the time comes for action.

beyond many of the differences in how they each saw the world. They adored one another. It seemed to me they played as much as they worked, but when they were working they were serious about the outcome. My mom used to say, "When your daddy gets something wrong it breaks his heart. But when he gets it right, all is right with the world."

LIMITATIONS IN RELATIONSHIPS

Ones tend to overdo their effort to do things well—they overthink, overtalk, overevaluate, and overplan. This tendency to go over-the-top is due to their honest and deep desire to do things right. Ones are wonderfully responsible people, but when they take on too much responsibility for themselves and for others, they may experience some anger and resentment. So it's really important that Ones minimize the temptation to overdo by stopping to ask the question: "What is mine to do?"

Most of us are just not as observant as Ones. They are aware of themselves, other people, and their surroundings. This kind of awareness can be a gift for everyone, but it can also become limiting. Remember, Ones are the only people on the Enneagram who actually believe every step of a task should be done correctly, so they will have to be careful that the high standards they set for themselves don't become unreasonable expectations for others. Ones also need to learn to recognize when things are good enough and leave it at that.

I often encourage Ones to be mindful of the times when they take things too seriously. When a One becomes too sober about too many things—too thoughtful or too aware—they can be hard on other people and themselves, and they find it hard to lighten up, even when they sense they should.

THE PATH TOGETHER

On Easter Sunday a few years ago, our four children and their children all went with us to the church where my husband, Joe, served as pastor. For some reason, all of the grandchildren wanted to sit by me—maybe because they know Easter services last longer than most and I almost always have candy in my purse. It was a hot day in Dallas, and I had on a pastel linen jacket, which by late morning was quite wrinkled.

Joe was starting his sermon when my grandson Noah, who was eight years old, punched me on the arm and whispered, "Grams, is your iron broken?"

"No, darlin', why?"

"Your jacket looks terrible! Why didn't you iron it?"

I love all seven of my grandchildren with a heart full of hope that in some way my work with the Enneagram will make their world better. I'm not certain of their Enneagram numbers, but I'm quite sure Noah is a One. I gently replied to him, "Oh, you mean the wrinkles? This jacket is linen and linen always wrinkles. But everyone knows that so it's okay."

He had been quiet for a few minutes more when he nudged me again and said, "I'll bet Granddaddy is really embarrassed. It just doesn't look good, Grams."

Still whispering, I explained that Joe wasn't embarrassed and that Noah should be quiet and try to listen. I focused my attention on the pulpit hoping Noah would too, but he just couldn't take his eyes off of me and my wrinkled jacket. Finally, he got up and moved all the way to the far end of the pew. I suppose he thought it was the only place he could find peace.

Perhaps the lesson here for Ones is this: If you can't stand what you're looking at, it might help to move.

But the lesson for those of us who love Ones is to remind them to be kind to themselves—simply because it's the *right* thing to do.

RELATIONSHIPS *for* ONES

After all is said and done ...

Perhaps more than any other number, Ones struggle to accept the reality that there are certain things they must accept. Here are some other things for Ones to keep in mind:

You can ...

- have people in your life who "get you"—other Ones, or others who understand Ones.
- be gracious when other people don't do things the way you think they should be done.
- seek perfection, but you can't have it. Perfection is momentary, then something shifts and everything changes.
- make every effort to leave everything better than you found it, though you can't do it alone.

But you can't ...

- have inner peace if you continue to commit to an ever-rising set of internal standards for yourself.
- accurately measure your own goodness and value based on the constant chatter of the inner critic.
- live in a world where everyone attends to details in the same ways that you do.
- change how others see.
- expect other numbers to achieve perfection as you define it. That isn't just a matter of preference; it's how they see, and it's not going to change, no matter what you do or say.

So you'll need to accept that ...

- your way is not the only right way.
- some things—perhaps many things—are good enough.
- you need to stop working so you and others can rest.
- you are good—*really* good—just as you are.

RELATIONSHIPS *with* ONES

Since Ones often doubt their value and worthiness, they need to hear and believe that they are good and that they are loved. The inner critical voice is, in some ways, part of the relationship too. Here are some other ways to grow your relationships with Ones:

- Ones tend to offer more criticism than praise, so they will likely be more verbal about what you do wrong than about the things you get right. Teach them that praise often works better for you.

- Work to avoid making Ones feel like they have to prove to you that they are good or that they are doing things right.

- Be careful and gentle when you point out their mistakes—it can easily be overwhelming for the One if you come on too strong.

- Admit your mistakes in the relationship.

- Value their diligence and honor their high standards without getting caught up in either one. Both represent *their* way of seeing the world, not yours.

- Ones appreciate equity—they work hard and they expect the same from you.

- Ones need you to be loyal and trustworthy because they are.

- When you're in conflict with a One, let them know that you want to resolve it. They will need to hear that you are committed to working things through.

- Ones like to be appreciated for all of their effort, so they tend to like cards and notes and accolades and small gifts.

- Ones like order, so it will help if you honor that in the spaces you share with them.

- Be careful about off-handed remarks and teasing. Ones are very sensitive to the slightest criticism.

- Support vacations and time away from work and responsibilities, encourage downtime at home, and help them verbally process their day.

- When things get contentious, it's often about the One's way of seeing the world and not really about you at all. In those moments, the only thing you can do is wait until something shifts—either in them or in the situation.

2s

YOUR FEELINGS OR MINE?

A few years ago, I struck up a conversation with Hunter, whose vocation is a surprising combination of full-time pastor and part-time attorney. Like me, Hunter is a Two, so our conversation quickly centered on what we both like best about being Twos. "Well, the thing about practicing law," he said, "is that you're always looking for the one thing that the person hasn't told you. Whenever a client comes into your office, there's a big missing fact that they will not put on the table. So you are trying to intuit what isn't being shared—while you are listening to what people are telling you, you're discerning what they're leaving out."

That was certainly familiar territory for me, so I asked, "What about the same gift in your work as a pastor?" After a pause, Hunter admitted that it was complicated. On the one hand, being relational and geared to help others makes him uniquely gifted as a pastor. But on the other hand, Twos can have terrible boundaries and can find themselves "entangled in people's lives in ways that are not helpful to them or to us."

Then Hunter confessed, "The other thing that I would say is hard is that being a pastor can be a very lonely job. It lacks mutuality. For Twos, the relationship is always about the other person. You can't say what you want or feel because it could cause a disconnect." He went on to describe the isolation he experiences in his work—finding himself so engrossed in helping others that he loses himself.

"It's very difficult to know who I am when I'm alone. I want responses from other people that show that they appreciate me, but I don't want to ask for them, and if I do receive accolades from others I have no idea how to handle them. So the most complicated time of my work week as a pastor is about twenty minutes after I've preached a sermon. After the service, I desperately want a line to form and to hear people say, 'That was the best sermon I've ever heard,' but when I do hear that I can't trust it. So, I wouldn't say I actually enjoy it. It's like something I need that I am not able to savor. I need people to affirm me and my work, but I can't receive it so I've learned to deflect it. I simply redirect the conversation so it's about the other person and not about me."

What's Going on Here?

When you listen to other people's stories, do you wonder what they're leaving out?

Does Hunter's impulse to sense and respond to the needs and desires of other people sound familiar?

Why do you think Hunter believes that saying what he needs or wants or feels will cause a disconnect between him and another person?

Do you trust affirmation when it's offered? Why or why not?

Twos read the world with feelings. They connect to other people by picking up on their feelings and respond by doing something. They express emotions so easily you might think those feelings are their own, but that is seldom the case. Twos feel the feelings of others and find it very difficult to tell you what *they* actually feel. That's a hard truth with many implications for a relationship with a Two.

THE WORLD OF TWOS

For Twos, everything is relational. They make their way in the world by connecting with almost every person they encounter and by building a relationship with everyone they can engage on a regular or semi-regular basis. It's the way Twos know themselves. I was probably fifty years old before I introduced myself as "Suzanne Stabile," rather than by relationships such as "I am Joe's wife" or "I am Doc and Sue's adopted daughter," "I am Joel's mom" or "I am Will's grandmother."

Twos don't know who they are unless they get that information from someone else. One Two said, "When I go on a silent retreat, I literally can't think about anything but my relationships with my husband, my kids, my friends, and my colleagues. When I pray, I pray for other people. When I read, I think about how what I've read will be helpful to someone else. With such a focus on others, there is little energy left for knowing ourselves, so the hardest questions anyone ever asks me are 'What do you want?' and 'What are you feeling?' I literally don't know the answers, because even though I come across as a feeling person, like most Twos, I seldom know or express my own."

PRIDE. Twos believe that everyone is their responsibility in one way or another, and they take pride in meeting the needs of others. That's the Two's passion (or sin). In our conversation, Hunter said, "I can remember as a child having the thought of being absolutely devastated if someone didn't like me. That's the pride of being the best, the most helpful, and the most loved." Don Riso and Russ Hudson define the Two sin of pride as "the inability or unwillingness to acknowledge one's own needs and suffering while tending to the needs of someone else." This inability to identify their own needs while navigating the world causes Twos a great deal of pain.

A lot of personal work is required to change this pattern for two very important reasons. The first is that Twos generally don't see themselves as *worthy* of needing anyone's help.

The second reason is a bit more complex: Twos are afraid to express a need or desire because if no one responds, they fear they won't be able to manage the pain and disappointment. But relationships require reciprocity, so Twos have to learn to ask directly for what they want or need and then they must cultivate the grace to receive it. When they don't, they often resort to manipulation. Their connections with others take on a dishonest quality that isn't satisfying for anyone. Saying, "I wish I didn't have to cook dinner tonight," is not the same thing as "Do you mind if we go out to dinner tonight? I'm tired and just don't feel like cooking."

You can see how this gift for manipulation can lead to Twos seeing themselves as martyrs. And this kind of manipulation and martyrdom is accompanied by anger due to unmet expectations and a feeling of being taken for granted. But none of this is necessary; healthy Twos know how to name and then ask others for what they need.

THE VULNERABILITY OF GENEROSITY. As a Two, I have a lot of practice with giving. In an honest effort through the years to examine the altruism of my generosity, I discovered that being the *giver* often feels like a place of strength. But there is a vulnerability in generosity that sneaks up on Twos at the most unexpected times.

> Twos often assume that others need their help and protection.
>
> 2

When the desire to give is multiplied many times over, limitations begin to show themselves and Twos struggle to keep up with the commitments they make to others. They volunteer easily, but the satisfaction of giving wears off when the expectations from others outweigh the gratitude Twos receive. After initiating a relationship with someone, Twos struggle to disengage. It's an ongoing dilemma for them.

The other person, having received lavish attention from a Two for some time, is usually very confused when suddenly the Two becomes somewhat distant and unavailable. From the perspective of the Two, they give until they're empty, and then they return to their own lives tired and lacking any energy to care for themselves. They feel unappreciated, taken for granted, tired, and afraid. Their fear is primarily because their self-worth is determined by their giving. If they have nothing left to offer, they struggle to know whether they have any value at all.

The problem is that Twos try to have relationships with everyone—servers in restaurants, the woman who grooms their dog, their plumber, everyone in their church, all of their coworkers, their neighbors—and some of those relationships will not or cannot be appropriate or healthy or reciprocal. When Twos begin to

> **2** Twos are more comfortable with affection than any other Enneagram number.

describe their feelings with words like drained, resentful, tired, and frustrated, that is often their way of asking for help.

DISCONNECTION FROM PRODUCTIVE THINKING. Twos make their way by reading the feelings of others and then doing something in response. They don't think about what they're experiencing, so the lack of productive thinking in situations and relationships doesn't show itself until Twos come to a full stop. The satisfying interplay between feeling and doing has a rhythm that is so comfortable for Twos, they are unaware of the cost of their overdoing, overgiving, over-relating, and underthinking. When Twos are experiencing a lot of anxiety and fatigue, it's usually a signal that they need to stop, consider all that they are involved in, discern what is theirs to do, appropriately pass on to others what is not theirs to do, and think about what's going on rather than continuing to react emotionally from their automatic desire to identify and meet the needs of others.

Several years ago, I was teaching a large group of Enneagram students at an event with Father Richard Rohr in Assisi, Italy. The session was going well, but early on I noticed a sour-faced man sitting about midway back in the audience. Every time I looked at him—and I couldn't keep myself from looking at him—he was either scowling or had no affect at all. I don't experience that very often when I'm teaching, so I was distracted and wondered why he didn't like what I had to say. The other participants seemed to be dialed in and enjoying my presentation, so I finally came to the conclusion that he didn't speak English. As the time passed I began to feel sorry for him, trapped in the middle of a row during a lecture and unable to understand what was being said.

At the break, I hurried through the crowd to catch him. Once I caught up with him I shouted, the way you do when you think someone doesn't speak the same language: loudly and obnoxiously. As I made headphone motions

Our Enneagram passions teach us lessons we need to learn.

with my hands, I said, "They have translators. German! French!"

He looked me in the eye and said, "I speak English."

I was so surprised. "Then why don't you react to anything I say? You don't laugh or scoff or even look away."

"Well, I don't like you and I don't like what you're saying."

In typical Two fashion I asked, "Why?"

Without any feeling, with the same flat affect and tone, he said, "I don't like anything about you."

Stunned by his abrasiveness, I stepped back and ran right into Father Richard, who had heard the entire exchange. He looked at me compassionately and said, "Suzanne, you're still going after the one." Then, with an upturned hand, he said, "You have two hundred people in the palm of your hand. Why are you ignoring them and focusing on him?"

Of course, Father Richard was right. I was blinded by my feeling of rejection from that one individual and did not stop to think about the room full of people who were engaged. I gave away all of my power to this one disgruntled man. Twos often go after the one they don't have, risking relationships with others in the process.

In order to avoid an innate sense of loneliness, Twos tend to avoid questions that ask, Who do I belong to? Am I worth belonging to anyone? Is anyone going to be there for me when I really need them? When these questions bubble up to the surface, the Two response is usually to cover their loneliness by doubling their efforts to help. Unfortunately, that assumes the other person is always needy.

The truth is, I bank relationships and I bank favors, and for the most part I do all of that unconsciously. This year I've allowed myself to wonder, "What is available to me that I'm not withdrawing from my emotional bank?" To my surprise, there is a sufficient supply available.

2s and Others

1s: Since Twos always put relationship before strategy, they will struggle some with Ones. But with a One wing, Twos can appreciate a respect for order. That common ground is a place to begin.

2s: Twos with a Two struggle to know who will lead, when, and how. Twos are other-referenced, so the focus may be on others outside of the relationship with needs to be met.

3s: Twos and Threes are both image conscious, so their perception of how they are seen can determine their choices. However, Twos want to be wanted and Threes want to be loved for who they are and not merely for what they do. The expressions of those desires can be misleading. So in this relationship, enjoy the comradery but respect the difference.

4s & 8s: Twos do well with Fours and Eights even if they are a little uncomfortable around them. Fours and Eights are authentic, something Twos need.

5s: Twos struggle in this relationship because Fives prefer to keep their thoughts, plans, and ideas to themselves, Twos need to wait until Fives are ready to share information about their lives.

Twos have a hard time trusting people when they say, "I'm not going anywhere," or "You can count on me if you need me." I have always thought, *Yeah . . . maybe. Maybe you will be there for me.* But in my heart, I have struggled to believe I'm worth it. All I can say for sure is that I have learned that I am much less alone than I suspected.

Twos probably have more and deeper connections with people than other numbers tend to have, and yet it doesn't seem to satisfy. So I'm learning that if affirmation isn't working, it's because it isn't really affirmation that I'm looking for. It's belonging. And the next step is believing that I can trust the belonging that is available to me.

Twos need to look for happiness from the inside out as opposed to expecting it to always come from somewhere or someone outside of themselves. Twos are really good at offering a place for belonging to other people but not to themselves. Healthy relationships demand that you have a strong sense of yourself when you're alone. If Twos ask, Who am I when I'm alone? they will be surprised by what they discover. Yes, Twos want to make sure everyone has a seat at the table, but they need to be aware that they need to take their seat as well.

STRESS AND SECURITY

When Twos are in a healthy space, they are generous but also playful and nurturing. They make other people comfortable, they are aware when others feel left out or marginalized in any way, and they will usually find ways to meet you where you are. They're accepting and they seldom adhere to insider/outsider thinking and behavior.

When they're trapped in a pattern of unhealthy responses, Twos are controlling and possessive and insecure. Jealousy becomes a problem when they fear they might lose the attention and affection of someone they love. One of my students who is a Two said, "When I'm in that unhealthy pattern of behavior, I am either overinvolved or underinvolved— I'm either meddling and bossy or I just cut people off. I think it's because sometimes I don't know how to be with people in a space that is good and healthy and interdependent."

Twos have such a strong desire for connection that they can easily be too personal and just too much for others.

2

When Twos start to feel separated from others, they create circumstances where they will be needed. If you're in relationship with a Two, a clue that they are feeling stressed is when they begin to complain about their health. Their repressed feelings can even cause physical symptoms, and then they pull others in with self-pity. The truth is, an offended Two can change the mood of an entire group of people without ever saying a word. I suspect this is where the saying on the refrigerator magnet originated: "If mama ain't happy, ain't nobody happy."

In stress, Twos go to Eight, which means they have more self-confidence and they care less about what other people think. They find that they can say no to things that are not theirs to do and they have more patience with process and personal differences. When Twos are feeling secure they have access to some Four energy, awareness, and behavior, so they can be accepting of their own feelings. They might even be able to admit that in fact they *don't* love everybody. In this place of security, they discover some self-worth that isn't connected to helping others, and they can even focus inward at times. It is a good and necessary move toward better self-care.

LIMITATIONS IN RELATIONSHIPS

Perhaps the main limitation in relationships for Twos is that they are involved in too many relationships. That causes a host of problems: they don't have the time or the energy to attend to all of the people in their lives, so they end up apologizing for no-fault situations. Ironically, the people Twos love the most get the leftovers—Twos trust that their closest relationships will always be there, so they short them on time and attention. Twos give too much to others and return to their own lives feeling tired, empty, and taken for granted, which leaves very little time or energy to care for themselves.

Twos assume that any problem in a relationship is their fault. They are very slow to leave relationships and generally fall into the trap of believing they can make a big enough

> You can't take care of yourself without the number you go to in stress.

commitment to cover both sides. They can't. Sometimes it's healthy to leave a relationship, but Twos need to accept that it won't feel good, even when the benefits of ending relations with someone else are obvious.

THE PATH TOGETHER

When Andy Andrews passed away, people sent his son all sorts of letters and cards describing experiences and memories they had of him. One woman shared a story from thirty years prior, when she and her husband had visited Andy at his home in North Carolina.

After breakfast, your father asked if I wanted to go to his garden and see his blueberry plants. It was a hot summer morning, and on the way to the garden we passed a lovely water feature. Andy asked me to come over to see it. The water came down the rocks, then fell into a depression in a larger rock, forming a small pool, and then it fell into a larger pool at its base.

Lining the edges of the smaller pool were honeybees, from the hive your dad had. They were drinking water, like cattle around a pond. Your dad said to me, "Did you know that you can pet honeybees when they're drinking water? And there's a really good chance they won't sting you." I thought he was joking, but then he walked over to them, and started to stroke their furry backs. They just kept drinking.

As I drove back to my home that evening, I said to my husband, "What kind of man pets bees?"

For years I didn't have an answer. But I have some land of my own now, and a hive of bees. When I heard your dad died, the answer to my question was clear: a man who pets honeybees is a man who believes that it's worth the risk of a sting for the possibility of a connection.

That possibility is the primary motivation for Twos, so it's a lifelong challenge for them to accept that not every connection is intended to become a relationship.

RELATIONSHIPS *for* TWOS

After all is said and done ...

We live in an affluent culture with an illusion of control. We have a sense that with some work, we can make things what we want them to be. But Twos have to learn to let others make their own free choices and then either suffer or celebrate the consequences.

Here are some other things for Twos to keep in mind:

You can ...

- learn to accept that healthy relationships are reciprocal, and learn the value of both receiving and giving.

- learn to meet your needs from the inside out instead of from the outside in.

- learn to commit to fewer relationships and enjoy them more.

But you can't ...

- expect other Enneagram numbers to sense and meet your needs before you name them.

- have healthy relationships with more people than your life can accommodate. Every yes you say in one relationship requires a no in another.

- experience lasting peace until you discover that you are capable of identifying and taking care of your own feelings and many of your own needs. That doesn't threaten your relationships. It will make them better.

- find the security you look for in relationships until you learn to find satisfaction in doing some things independently.

So you'll need to accept that ...

- other people are meeting your needs in their own way. It may not be the way you would do it, but it's just as good.

- you are well loved.

- you are worthy of being loved and you are wanted.

RELATIONSHIPS *with* TWOS

Twos are very perceptive about what other people want or need from them. At the same time they are usually disconnected from what they need and want from others. One key to relationships with Twos is to help bridge the gap. Here are some other things to keep in mind:

- Twos experience anxiety when they recognize that they are feeling their own feelings. They don't know a lot about how to act on their own behalf.

- Try to help Twos find a way to share with you what they honestly feel.

- Twos can only process verbally. They don't *think* things through—they *talk* their way through them. You can avoid so much misunderstanding by keeping this in mind.

- Don't trust their answer when they say they're fine or good. Press a little deeper.

- Twos want honest feedback, but they take everything personally. So if you say, "I don't like your spaghetti recipe," they hear, "I don't like you." You don't need to remind them that it isn't personal; they know that and they're trying to outgrow that way of thinking.

- In an intimate relationship, Twos need to hear you say, "I'm here and I'm not going anywhere. There's nothing you need to *do*, there's nothing you need to *be*, and there's nothing you need to help me with. I love you for you."

- Encourage Twos to let you address your own feelings.

- Twos need a partner who is demonstrative with affection. It is very reassuring.

- Twos need a partner who wants to meet and know their friends.

- While Twos are happy to be second in command, be sure to acknowledge their contribution.

- Try to have patience when Twos are overly concerned regarding their relationships with other people. Your impatience with that reality will only add to their insecurity.

- Anger or disproportionate emotional responses usually signal unmet needs.

3s

BEING EVERYONE
BUT MYSELF

*J*ake, a colleague of mine, died unexpectedly at the age of forty. When I arrived at the funeral, the parking lot was full and the church was packed. I found an aisle seat with some people I had met but didn't know well. As I settled in, a woman approached the lectern to speak about her long relationship with the man whose life we were there to celebrate. The more she talked, the more I began to wonder if I was attending the right funeral—I even checked the bulletin to make sure—because I simply didn't recognize the person she was talking about.

The next speaker told a couple of stories about his relationship with Jake, saying how much he would miss his gentle spirit (something I had never experienced) and his availability to be helpful any time he could (another thing I had not found to be true). Two more speakers followed, and both described a person I didn't recognize. At the funeral and many times since, I've wondered how it could be possible for Jake to somehow be all of those people I heard eulogized and remembered that day.

The Enneagram's wisdom has a simple answer.

What's Going on Here?

How could someone be seen and remembered so differently by various people?

Have you ever been in a similar situation—for example, a conversation about someone in which you and another person have completely different takes?

Would attendees of your funeral have a similar experience to my experience at Jake's funeral?

When we look at this story through the lens of the Enneagram, it is another reminder of how unique we are as personality types and as human beings. Threes have the gift and the burden of being able to adapt themselves to any person or group. They work very hard to be who they think you want them to be. They can adapt quickly but they can only inhabit one role at a time, so casual relationships suffer when Threes are with people from several different parts of their lives at the same time. Personal relationships suffer because they don't allow others to know who they are underneath all that they can accomplish. And intimate relationships suffer the most. Those with whom Threes have the most intimate relationship may not ever get to know them for who they truly are. As a result, Threes keep believing that they are loved for what they do instead of who they are.

THE WORLD OF THREES

Even though Threes are in the Feeling Triad along with Twos and Fours, they quickly replace feeling with doing and thinking. Threes sometimes struggle to read the feelings of others, but the greater struggle is to read their own feelings. Sometimes Threes know what they're feeling, but they just don't want to deal with it.

To further complicate things, Threes find it hard to distinguish their personal feelings from the feelings that come with a position or role. Activity is a form of control, so at an early age, Threes decided to control their environment by doing. Threes get more done on any given day than every other Enneagram number, with the exception of Eights.

Threes are personable but they are seldom *personal*, even with those who are closest to them. Because Threes are feeling repressed and because they want to be appropriate, they sometimes offer the appearance of feelings they aren't experiencing. A college professor who is a Three acknowledges that so much of what he does is about appearance: "I want to be seen as competent and capable, and I want people to note that I do the right thing at the right time, and that I do it successfully." Unfortunately, feelings get wrapped into this impulse for image management: "What I'm saying is that I can perform when it comes to feelings too.

Competition motivates Threes. 3

I'm not intentionally deceptive and inauthentic—it just happens." But control is an illusion, particularly in relationships. With such a focus on doing, Threes neglect *being*, and end up disregarding some of the most important elements in any relationship: being present, being who they really are, being with others, and being available.

Threes are enamored with the future and its possibilities: more success, more achievement, and more affirmation. So they have a self-imposed, ever-changing need to create the most appropriate image for any given meeting or event or introduction. For that reason, they find what's happening in the present moment to be mostly a distraction, and they see little value in looking back. At their best, Threes can morph into whatever the situation requires. But this can also be true when they're at their worst.

> There are valuable attributes associated with every number.

I spent three days recently working with an advanced Enneagram group talking about balance, including trying to find some balance in our lives with regard to the past, present, and future. On Saturday morning while Amy, a young Four, was talking about how much she treasures looking back, even when it's painful, Larry, who is a One, responded, "It's all I can do to manage what's happening right now." An older woman who is a strong Three seemed perplexed as they each explained their struggles with time. Her response was, "I can barely relate to what you're saying. It's already Monday in my world!"

For the most part, Threes have good boundaries, but they don't recognize limits—for themselves or for others. They seem to have an unending supply of energy, and yet they are often tired because they don't know when to stop. Perhaps that's why they take so many shortcuts, including in their relationships, because sometimes getting things done takes precedence over doing things right. While that approach works for relationships with other Threes, it certainly creates problems with other numbers: with Ones who value perfection, and Twos who value relationships, and Sixes who struggle with the Threes' lack of forethought.

Most Threes want to be the star. They believe that if you can't win first place, you shouldn't enter the race. If you can't lead, you shouldn't follow. If you don't know the right answer, you should be quiet. And if you can't

3s and Others

1s: Threes and Ones are both all about getting things done, but Threes accomplish that by cutting corners whereas Ones believe every step of a task should be done correctly. It is helpful if Threes can be patient with the One's desire to check every step and engage in even a brief conversation about what was accomplished together.

2s: Threes can be very effective with Twos both personally and professionally because Twos focus on people while Threes focus on the task. If there is mutual respect, your gifts can be complementary. The challenge for Threes is to be patient with the emotional and verbal processing of the Two.

3s: When a Three is with another Three, everything seems possible. It isn't. So it's a gift when you choose to be the one who offers a more cautious voice.

4s: In a relationship with a Four, emotions will be the trigger. Fours overvalue feelings and Threes don't value them enough. Until Threes develop a Four wing, this connection will be tricky.

5s: Threes and Fives have great gifts to exchange if each is open. Threes are driven to action. Fives need more downtime. You can learn from each other.

6s: Threes love success, but Sixes don't trust it. They find the Three's eagerness to make a good impression and demonstrate their prowess phony and off-putting. This disconnect requires a lot of bridging, but it's possible. Sixes find satisfaction in group experiences where they are not the leader. Since Threes share a line on the Enneagram with Sixes, they need that behavior to experience holistic healing. Sometimes healing only comes when we follow.

7s & 8s: Threes, Sevens, and Eights are all very strong —none of them want to be vulnerable. Threes provide, Eights protect, and Sevens avoid, and all three numbers are dismissive of feelings. These numbers all get along, but they *all* have to commit to some reality checks.

9s: Threes do well with Nines if the two share a common value system. Threes tend to want to *make* things happen. Nines hang back and *allow* things to happen. Both are good, depending on the situation. Nines often need the energy and direction of Threes, and Threes need a Nine's sense of holy delay.

make a good impression, then don't make an impression at all.

Our granddaughter Elle, who I'm fairly certain is a young Three, had a heartbreaking experience in first grade. Just before the Christmas holidays, the librarian read a story to Elle's class. In the story, Santa Claus was a fictional character. Elle waited until the teacher finished reading and then she stood up to defend the existence of Santa Claus. Elle told the whole class not to worry, explaining that the story wasn't about the *real* Santa Claus. The other children in her class snickered and gave her a hard time for still believing in Santa.

After Elle tearfully recounted the story to her dad, he told her how sorry he was that she found out about Santa at school. "I know it must be hard to give up believing that Santa is real. But it will be okay. Mommy and I will still be good Santas for you."

Elle shot back, "I'm not crying about Santa! I'm crying because I felt like such a failure for believing in him in the first place!"

Threes cannot tolerate feeling uninformed or inadequate. This is a result of their propensity for comparison and competition. Comparison is a natural way of seeing for Threes. Every bit of information they take in gets sorted into one of two categories: "what is" and "what could be." When I ask Threes to share stories that represent the best of their number, I'm often met with hesitation. I can usually get them to admit to waiting until they hear from others to determine whether their story will measure up.

Most Threes are very competitive, but unlike Eights, who enjoy competition because the energy is high, Threes are in it to win. When you think about how much competition awaits us every day, the pressure for Threes is obvious. Threes who commit to Enneagram work open themselves up to the reality that although they want do their part, they get caught in wanting what they bring to the table to be the best. But they learn necessary lessons when they take the risk whether theirs is the best or not.

THE NEED TO REFRAME FAILURE. When they experience failure, Threes quickly reframe it as a partial victory. And if that doesn't work, they distance themselves from whatever went wrong and attribute problems to factors outside of their purview.

A flight attendant recently told me a story about serving beverages on one of her first flights. As a trainee, she thought the bloody marys and margaritas included the alcohol in the can. Several of the passengers who were drinking told her they thought their drinks were a bit light and asked if they might have another. She complied. One insisted that his drink had no alcohol in it, but she convinced him that it had the regular amount and that it probably didn't taste the same because it was a different brand. Another asked for a double, but she didn't think that would be wise. When she served him his drink, she talked him into thinking it was much stronger than his previous drink.

After the beverage service was completed, the supervising flight attendant who had to fill out the inventory for the alcohol realized that the trainee had, in fact, been serving drinks with no alcohol.

I asked the flight attendant if she was reprimanded by her supervisor. "Well," she explained, "it was the flight from LA to Vegas, and I just told her that those who ordered the drinks were young and had probably already had enough to drink. I explained that I felt like it was our responsibility to care for them appropriately and that I thought it would be better for everyone on the flight if I didn't serve them more alcohol at that time."

"Did you get away with that?" I asked.

"Yes. I pointed the drinkers out to her. They were content.

Two were sleeping, and one who had been fairly rambunctious when he boarded was quietly sipping his virgin bloody mary."

Threes don't like to be wrong, so they justify their behavior by reframing the story—and they are good at it, often believing the story themselves.

IMAGE AND SELF-PROTECTION. Threes intuitively use image as a way of assuring their place in relationships with other people. At some point in childhood they came to believe that it was not okay to have their own feelings and their own identity. In relationships with family and authority figures, Threes were convinced that it would be better to put their feelings aside and become what people around them expected and would applaud as desirable and successful. So they began to develop their innate ability to be whatever is called for. They can belong to as many as fifteen to twenty groups, from family to professional to voluntary, and be the poster child for each of them. It's a remarkable gift that is difficult to manage in a healthy way.

> Each number's passion or sin can sometimes be so strong that it defines their behavior.

When we love Threes they have no idea which part of them we love, so it's difficult for them to accept that we love *all* the parts of them. I received a text from a well-known artist who I suspect is a Three. While celebrating her sixty-first birthday in the Sacre Coeur Basilica in Paris, she wrote, "I am finally able to believe that I am welcome at God's Table. All of the me's are welcome."

If you are in a relationship with a Three, it is very important that you understand that every "me" they present to you or to someone else is an effort to give you what they think you want because they believe that if they offered you what was behind the image, it would be neither lovable nor desirable. It's troubling to know that such lovely and lovable people struggle to believe that they have value as they are. Imagine the vulnerability of that in a relationship. Twos hide their vulnerability with being needed and helpful, Fours hide it by pulling you toward them and then pushing you away, and Threes hide it by overachieving.

DECEIT. A Three's behavior is seamless when they are shapeshifting to please others, which may appear to be a gift, but in reality it is a complex problem because they lose touch with who they are, what they think, and how they really feel. When Threes focus on the bottom line of success and achievement, when they cut corners, and when they don't read feelings well (their own and the feelings of others), it not only creates misunderstanding, but they miss out on so much. The greatest loss occurs when they begin to believe that their "constructed image" is who they are. That is the sin or passion of deceit—Threes deceive *themselves.*

More often than not, work is the center of a Three's life. It takes great effort and self-awareness to

3 Because Threes conform to each relationship they're in, they have difficulty expressing consistent values.

change that, and the change isn't usually supported by the boss. However, because of grace, I suppose, sometimes personal experience causes Threes to reexamine their values and what they give themselves to.

A friend who is a Three shared an example of this with me: "Suzanne, there are things I value that are at odds with the organization I work for. One example is centered on the needs and the rights of my brothers and sisters who are in the LGBTQ community. I have a son who is gay, and where I work offers no safety or support for me to talk about that. At times, I feel like a fraud." Removing the masks we all wear to make our way in the world can have significant consequences— some good, some less so.

In my experience with Threes, transformative change for the sake of the relationships that matter the most almost always has a negative effect on the relationships that matter the least. It's very courageous work.

STRESS AND SECURITY

Threes are on the central triangle of the Enneagram along with Nines and Sixes. At their most unhealthy, they appear to be desperate for attention, demanding to be noticed and encountered, bragging about successes and often embellishing their role. If that fails, they get angry with anyone who doesn't believe the story they tell, and they can be punitive and destructive. Remember, Threes are highly and visibly competitive.

In stress, Threes move to Nine, which helps them mediate their competitive drive. With some Nine behavior on board, Threes are more open to other people and their ideas and tend to be more honest with themselves. They're able to rest a bit and relax, allowing their competitive energy to stand down. They still want to be noticed, but the need for that is not as intense, and they are better at engaging with others.

When they feel secure, Threes have access to some of the best parts of Six. In this move, Threes are much more aware of others. They aren't quite so sure of themselves, allowing them to slow down and collaborate in both professional and personal relationships. This is also the place where Threes are much more aware of their desire to connect to something or someone who is bigger than they are, rather than relying on their own strengths.

LIMITATIONS IN RELATIONSHIPS

Threes are highly valued in Western culture, where we prize youth, efficiency, achievement, and success. They work long hours without complaining. Threes tell me that vacations are very difficult for them due to technology that allows them to stay in touch and work while they're away. Business culture values employees who don't need downtime and appreciates the idea of always moving forward. That's good news for Threes.

But the downside of being a Three in the West is that our culture values and applauds the very traits that inhibit meaningful transformation; what serves Threes well professionally can be disastrous to personal relationships. When Threes regularly go to work early and stay late, their relationships suffer. When they consistently miss their children's activities because of projects or work, relationships suffer. If they aren't present with those they love, both physically and emotionally, relationships suffer.

Threes begin relationships with a storybook idea of what the relationship will be. The truth is that all relationships are messy and unpredictable, so when this reality hits Threes usually try to turn the relationship into what it could be by setting goals and making lists. At that point, the relationship becomes a task to be completed. If Threes cannot slow down, they will find it very hard to be affected by intimate feelings, leading to all sorts of negative consequences for their relationships.

Too often, Threes substitute ideas *about* emotions for the real thing. This approach only works in a relationship with a partner who is also willing to repress their feelings. Threes' orientation is toward fixing things, so they may be impatient or dismissive with someone who wants to be heard, like a Six, or with someone who processes verbally, like a Two. Threes are often intolerant of darker emotions, but unless Threes can learn to be present to the other person's feelings and their own, the relationship will surely be compromised.

When talking about relationships, a middle-aged Three told me,

I value intimacy, but on my terms—in small doses and when I am not in the middle of doing something. The irony is I want others to take care of me and support me. But it's hard for me to have the emotional energy to do the same in return. Others can know that I offer support and love by *doing* things for them. I know I cannot only show love by what I do, but it is a concrete way of expressing how I feel about others.

But intimate connections with others cannot be determined solely by one member of the party, nor will they always happen at a conveniently appointed time. It is both unfair and non-productive to expect from someone else what you cannot give. At the same time, we can all learn to stretch ourselves in ways that are unfamiliar or uncomfortable for the care of another and the good of a valuable relationship. That's the challenge for Threes.

THE PATH TOGETHER

The truth about Threes is often hard for them to hear. Courtney Pinkerton is a holistic life coach, the founder of Bird in Hand Coaching, the author of *The Flourish Formula*, and one of my favorite Threes. She recently moved to Nicaragua with her husband and three children where they continue to make a difference in the world.

One evening found Courtney and her husband, Richard, walking on the beach. The sun was setting, the volcano was shrouded in a mist, and their bare feet left footprints in the black, volcanic sand. It seemed to Courtney like the perfect moment to set an intention with Richard for the next phase of their life together, so she inquired about his goals and desires. But he showed little interest, saying, "I am just really enjoying this moment: the movement of the lake, the mist, us together—all of it."

Richard's response made Courtney laugh, and upon later reflection, she said,

> In any love affair there are a multitude of parts to play: sometimes one is the dreamer, one is the doer. One the artist and the other manages the checkbook. Or one the life coach and the other the data guru. I don't think that these roles are bad in and of themselves as long as you stay nimble and don't get wedged in only one spot. It is good to take turns playing all the parts. And truthfully the roles we play in a partnership usually reflect the voices and human aspects we carry inside ourselves.

Threes are better equipped than any number on the Enneagram for playing all the parts—if and when they are able to honor who they are both inside and out.

RELATIONSHIPS *for* THREES

After all is said and done . . .

Threes contribute to the lives of other people by helping them define and reach their potential. Threes are quick and smart and they get things done. At the same time, as Richard Rohr says, the saddest number on the Enneagram is an unsuccessful Three. Perhaps it would be wise for Threes to expand their definition of success and recognize that others have a value system that may not match theirs.

Here are some other things for Threes to keep in mind:

You can . . .

- learn to move from emotional appearance to emotional depth.

- slow down, make friends, and enjoy activities that don't have an expected outcome or a tangible takeaway.

- learn to enjoy success without connecting it to your value as a human being.

But you can't . . .

- outrun your anxiety.

- set goals for other people. You can share a mutually agreed-upon goal for a relationship, but you will have to be careful that goals are compatible and realistic for both of you.

- protect yourself personally by becoming over-identified with groups or projects that you are a part of.

- be loved for who you are if you don't let people in and share at least some of your vulnerabilities.

So you'll need to accept that . . .

- your work is not your identity.

- roles are both deceptive and protective.

- you learn equally valuable lessons from both success and failure. As Father Rohr has said, "Success has very little to teach you after age thirty-five."

- there are no easy and quick solutions to hurt feelings and missed opportunities.

RELATIONSHIPS *with* THREES

Even though Threes appear to have endless energy since they measure their days and lives in productivity, underneath it all they are often exhausted. Let Threes know that it's not the image you love, but what's beneath it. Here are some other ways to build relationships with the Threes in your life:

- Don't assume that Threes have easy access to their feelings.

- Since their orientation to time is to the future, they're often distracted during conversations. It usually means something you've said has triggered some thoughts for them about something else and they unexpectedly prefer to pursue that line of thinking. Don't take the distraction personally.

- They won't be interested in rehashing things from the past.

- If they are not intentional, it will be hard for them to talk about what has happened or is happening in their lives at work.

- Threes don't lose well, so it's to their advantage to develop a way of seeing that is less dualistic, less focused on judging things as either good or bad, liked or disliked.

- Know that Threes want your approval and praise, and they really like it when you verbalize it.

- Try not to talk too much about negative things. Threes are very optimistic and they appreciate others who have a positive outlook.

- Avoid over-talking about your relationship.

- Threes come on strong, but they need you to be softer than they are.

- Verbalize your understanding of their struggle with image and their need to maintain it. At the same time, try to avoid encouraging image crafting and shape shifting.

- Threes need to be encouraged to identify and discuss their feelings. Do that, but once they share a thought or two, give them a break so they don't have to think about feelings for a while.

- Threes don't like to be interrupted when they are working on a project.

- Give Threes accurate and upfront information about what you need. They have a desire to meet your needs—they just struggle to know what they are.

4s

GO AWAY BUT DON'T LEAVE

*D*aphne had really enjoyed her dinner with Jane at their favorite bustling Japanese restaurant. So when she opened her mailbox two days later, she was surprised to see this letter from Jane. It was short but to the point:

Dear Daphne,

When we had dinner Tuesday night, you asked a couple of times if my new job was taking all my energy. And you were right, at least in part; the transition has required a lot from me. So, I don't have any extra energy, and that highlights the difference between us that's always there. You were so full of excitement about your new house and all the wonderful decorating you're doing, and so sad about the recurrence of your mom's breast cancer. I felt inadequate as a friend and unable to offer you much. I just don't have it right now, but I want to because when I have the stamina to offer myself to you it's pure magic. And we could both use a little magic.

For now, though, I need to focus on my new work. Know that I love you and let's reconnect after spring break.

Love,
Jane

Daphne put the letter down on the kitchen counter and felt a familiar rush of feelings. Disappointed. Sad. Confused. Rejected. Misunderstood. It was that same old thing: *I'm too much.* She wondered why Jane couldn't just say she was feeling really stretched and couldn't deal with much, instead of resorting to a five-week break.

Daphne was still upset by the time her husband, Mark, got home. As usual he hugged her and listened patiently and didn't try to talk her out of her feelings. He reminded her, as he had many times, that her passion and intensity are often misunderstood. What she intended as an invitation for connection seemed to be misunderstood as not leaving space for Jane. Daphne knew Mark was right. *It is what it is*, Daphne thought. *I'm sure Jane will call eventually.*

What's Going on Here?

What do you think surprised Daphne about Jane's letter?

How is emotional energy a factor in your relationships with other people?

Why do you think Jane wrote a letter instead of just saying something about her feelings at dinner?

In this relationship and others, what do you think creates the "magic" Jane mentions in her letter?

It is common for Fours like Daphne to hear that sometimes they are simply "too much"—even from people who care about them. The intensity of Fours' emotions, accompanied by unpredictable moods, requires understanding, compassion, patience, and an appreciation of the Fours' need for authenticity. In relationship with Fours, it can feel loving to suggest that they "normalize," but nothing could be further from the truth.

THE WORLD OF FOURS

Fours have a deep desire to be known, *really* known, for who they authentically are. Experience has taught them that most people don't take the time to get to know others, much less understand them. And that is true more often than not for Fours. When I talk to Fours about their relationships and their desire to be known, they consistently share two things. First, many people have abandoned them—they've experienced unexplained endings in relationships. And second, others often tell them that they are too much or too complicated. Despite the pain of relationships, Fours consistently pick themselves up and try again.

As children, Fours came to believe that there was something fundamentally wrong with them. My dear friend Elizabeth tells me that when she was growing up, her parents were uncomfortable with any expression of feelings and frequently told her that she was too sensitive.

Elizabeth adored her first grade teacher, Bunny Shelton. At 4'10" with a beehive that added a foot to her height, Ms. Shelton was charismatic and beloved. So when Elizabeth received a lollipop from Ms. Shelton one day, she proudly told her parents that she was the only one to receive a lollipop *and* that it was a reward for being so special.

Unfortunately, lollipop day was the same day as parent-teacher conferences. When Elizabeth's parents thanked Ms. Shelton for the lollipop, they discovered that *all* the children had received a treat. Angry and embarrassed by their daughter's deceit, Elizabeth's parents ordered her to apologize to Ms. Shelton for lying. Her desire to feel special had caused her great shame. Elizabeth recognized this as a pattern in her life:

I think there is a lot to be said about children who are Fours who cannot express their feelings at home. They can't be themselves. They can't feel special. I think they try to capture some of what's lost by lying, but then they get caught and are shamed by it. I believe what follows is that Fours begin to confuse being special or unique with externalized specialness. I think if I could have been more nurtured through the expressions of my feelings, I could have taken more ownership in my own real essence or specialness.

It feels like the essence of who I am couldn't be received so I had to manufacture it. When you grow up

that way, you end up having to accept manufactured specialness or personality, but you trade your authenticity
for it.

Most of us want to offer the best we have in important relationships. Eights prefer to offer strength. For Twos, "best" is
whatever is personal. And for Fours, "best" requires genuineness. It can be hard for anyone to make room for authenticity. When you encounter a Four who is a little too emotional and overly invested in their own percep-

> **There are at least nine different understandings of what is "best" in relationships.**

tions, they are acting out this desire to be authentic and real.

In building or trying to maintain a relationship, Fours
often feel some tension between their desire to be seen and
understood as uniquely themselves and the *laissez faire* attitude some have about making connections. When Fours
adapt in order to belong, it feels like they're selling out. But
when they choose their more authentic selves, it can feel like
sacrificing what they long for the most—real relationship.

ENVY. The sin or passion identified with Fours is envy.
Envy is not jealousy. Fours don't want your job or your house
or your car. Instead, they long for your comfort in the world.
They feel that your life is less threatening and less complicated. They also want your happiness—or what they perceive as your happiness. Since they don't have those things,
they envy you. And their envy reminds them that they are

considerably different from most of the people they know, so they feel trapped. They want the predictability and comfort of your life, but at the same time they want an authentic life that isn't like yours or any other life. Fours long so deeply for what they don't have that they often miss what they do have.

All of this is a real challenge in relationships. It's hard to learn to be with someone who so desperately wants to be satisfied, and at the same time cannot seem to find satisfaction with what is. In the end, everyone feels like they're failing.

SHAME. Average Fours often use their energy to maintain a self-image based on feelings and daydreams and stories from the past. In doing so, they may miss more authentic feelings as they arise because they have a habit of creating and then sustaining moods that suit them at the time. Immature Fours may choose the role of victim in order to feel some sense of value when someone goes to the trouble of attending to their distress. All of this behavior is an effort to escape the *shame* that comes from believing that they don't measure up in some fundamental way. It often works, but only momentarily.

Fours are in the Heart Triad with Twos and Threes. All three numbers need to learn that who you really are has nothing to do with what people think of you and nothing to do with your past. When these three numbers encounter difficulties in their relationships, they all initially believe that the problem lies with them, that whatever went wrong must be their fault, and that they are inadequate in some way. They are convinced that if they could do more, be more, achieve more, be different, be someone else, or just be exceptional, then they would be lovable and therefore loved.

If you are in a relationship with a Two, Three, or Four, the big question is, *Who are you in a relationship with?* Sometimes it's the person they really are, but sometimes it's the person they're pretending to be. Even though the required shape-shifting and adapting is much harder for Fours than for Twos and Threes, there is great sadness when Fours try to be whoever you might love and want.

Keep in mind that the numbers in the Heart Triad substitute all kinds of reactions for the power of real feelings. Twos are careful to pay close attention to the feelings of others while ignoring their own. Threes find feelings to be burdensome and unpredictable, so even though they initially recognize them both in themselves and others, they quickly set them aside as unimportant and unnecessary. Fours want the same satisfaction Twos and Threes seem to get from their way of managing things. However, if there is a breech in a valued relationship, ordinary feelings and ordinary results will not suffice.

> **4** Sometimes Fours overshare, overexplain, and overtalk—creating a sense of obligation that others simply can't meet.

Fours exacerbate their feelings to accommodate their sense of loss. For example, someone like Daphne might respond to Jane's letter by going home, listening to sad music, watching sad movies, and looking at old pictures that recap the friendship. In doing so, she could fall deeper and deeper into a very gratifying sadness. For Fours, an extraordinary friendship or relationship should never be remembered in an ordinary way.

AVOIDING ORDINARINESS. Fours want to avoid being ordinary because it is one way they protect their authenticity. They often avoid what is current and conventional and what we might call normal, seeking instead to try to describe how they see the world. One Four told me, "I'm afraid of average and I do not see 'normal' as a goal." Think about the complexity of this reality in relationships. Fours want to fit in but can't—they feel slightly out of step all the time. When you're in a relationship with them and the two of you are socializing with friends or colleagues, there will be times when you feel the same way.

> It's our nature, regardless of our Enneagram number, to be drawn toward some things and to avoid others.

The truth is that Fours *are* very special people, but they don't always know it so they try too hard to create specialness. And the cost can be high. The irony is that there is no need to avoid being ordinary because Fours seldom are. But if they expend some of their energy to embrace the ordinary tasks of life and the predictable, average, everyday ways of being in the world, it can enhance their relationships.

STRESS AND SECURITY

When stressed, Fours fall to the unhealthy range of their number where excess is obvious, somewhat destructive, and strangely comforting. In this space, their self-awareness becomes self-indulgence. Their commitment to being authentic devolves into a stubborn attachment to being different. They can be somewhat pretentious, acting like they deserve more than they have, and they may pretend to be unavailable, hoping you will pursue them.

Because they repress doing, unhealthy Fours lack stamina and determination. With the added element of shame, they feel incapable of doing anything to change the status quo. This leaves Fours feeling a hopelessness that is difficult for others to address effectively. If you're close to a Four, you may experience a similar lack of hope when trying to help them.

In stress, Fours take on some Two behavior. They begin to focus outside of themselves, abandoning the inner landscape that has become myopic. Michelle, a pastor's wife and mother of three adolescent boys, explained that she was hypervigilant to emotion in other people when she was a child; she was almost certainly in stress and so went to Two as a survival strategy. She would think, *What is wrong with my mother? What is wrong with my father? What is wrong with the way they talk to each other? What's wrong with my older brother? My baby brother? And what's wrong with me?* As the daughter of a conservative Christian minister, she felt constrained by her family's theology and by the need to look good. Bouncing back and forth between wondering what was wrong with her and what was wrong with the people around her, she concluded that it must be about her because they were all the same and she was different. It took going to college and finding a mentor and a group of women friends for her to start feeling likeable.

On the positive side, when Fours have access to Two behavior, they can be more nurturing in their relationships. They adjust their focus to include an awareness of what's happening outside of themselves along with being aware of what's going on inside. It's a good space and it's good for relationships.

When Fours experience some security, they take on One behavior. They are more disciplined, more productive, and even more creative in this space. The One influence that is most helpful to Fours is the ability to have feelings without expressing them and without acting on them.

4s and Others

1s: Ones often struggle with repressed emotions, so Fours can teach Ones to connect to their feelings as opposed to being trapped in right/wrong thinking. Ones can help Fours identify when their feelings transition from authentic to self-indulgent.

2s: Twos pursue and Fours flee. That can cause dysfunction in relationships, so be careful.

3s: Fours have as many mood swings in an hour as others do in a week and are attentive to all of them, but Threes suspend feelings. That's a lot to work through, and yet it would be healthy for both to meet in the middle.

4s: Fours are a gift to one another, and yet there are potential problems. The fear of abandonment can be very difficult to manage, but it can also be a shared experience that each appreciates in the other.

5s: Fives need space and Fours need intimacy. That will have to be worked out in friendship and other significant relationships. Both do well with honest exchanges.

6s: Fours and Sixes both feel misunderstood in the culture, which can be good as long as they can avoid feeling misunderstood by one another.

It can be comforting for Fours to know that their loyal Six friends will stick with them, even through their fluctuating emotions.

7s: Fours and Sevens are opposites on the Enneagram. That has the potential to be good or extremely complicated, depending on the appreciation they each have for the half range of emotion they ignore. Sevens can learn from Fours that many good things happen in the darker side of emotion, and Fours can learn from Sevens to welcome and appreciate joy.

8s: Fours and Eights have very different views of the world and their place in it. But if the Eight can be emotionally vulnerable and the Four can avoid being dramatic, these two can build an interesting relationship. It requires honest communication, something that's true of all good relationships.

9s: The good news for Fours is that Nines stay. That is very comforting to Fours, who are often concerned about abandonment. But there are some problems: neither is good at taking responsibility for choices and personal behavior, both have unspoken expectations, and both avoid *doing*. This can be a tricky relationship.

When Fours can access some One behavior, they are much more successful in relating to others.

LIMITATIONS IN RELATIONSHIPS

Since the very best part of you is also the worst part of you, there's a fine line between really good and too much. Some numbers manage that better than others, and Fours are among those who struggle with it the most.

Fours find meaning best expressed through stories, symbols, liturgy, art, music, and tradition. We can all name Fours we know who offer something that is just a little different from your average fare. These brilliant human beings add so much color and depth and texture to our lives. At the same time, we often feel like we have to make room for Fours because there are always ten more layers beneath what we can see. While that's intriguing, it's often a limitation when it comes to seeking and building relationships.

Fours often approach me and say, "No one gets me." Years ago, when I first started teaching, I made the mistake of trying to convince them that they were wrong. Now I simply respond by saying, "That's true—very few people understand your way of seeing the world, and that will probably always be your reality."

The solution is complicated for Fours. The thought of conforming in order to fit in is surely a temptation; but this desire is also their greatest liability, because even if feeling somewhat isolated and alone is undesirable, being inauthentic is totally unacceptable to Fours.

Bob Dylan was perhaps the consummate Four: he combined his talent with his unique way of understanding the world and offered us some of the most stunning lyrics ever written as he helped others struggle through the chaos of the '60s. In his song "Positively 4th Street," he expresses the loneliness of a Four, and yet he honors his fidelity to authenticity at the same time.

> I wish that for just one time
> You could stand inside my
>   shoes
> And just for that one moment
> I could be you

Most of us really don't "get" Bob Dylan, but I think we can

> **Fours often struggle to work through problems, especially when they feel misunderstood (which is most of the time) or when the remedy feels ordinary.**

still find a way to connect with his music. And that's our best hope in relationship with Fours: to believe that they too are trying to find a way to come out and connect with us.

Fours often pursue relationships they can't have. I suspect the way they are drawn to unattainable relationships is a kind of misguided and probably unconscious form of self-protection. They seem to believe that if they pursue someone who is unavailable and they are unsuccessful, it will be less painful than desiring a relationship with someone who is available but who may not choose to make a connection with them.

What we see and the way we see also determines what we miss.

My youngest son, BJ, is a Four. As an eight-year-old boy soprano, his dream was to spend as much time as he could singing, and he had the privilege of doing that as a member of the Texas Boys Choir. The forty boys in that choir performed together, went to school together, traveled together, grew up together, and knew exactly what buttons to push to hurt one another. BJ struggled to believe he really belonged because he could never connect with the boys he most wanted to connect with. Belonging came later in life, in part because he's a Four and in part because he's BJ, but his most obvious limitation in building relationships was his stubborn desire to be important to those who were unavailable.

Like BJ, Fours desire belonging more than any other number and live with the illusion that someone else can complete them. Oftentimes when average or immature Fours experience belonging as a possible reality, they sabotage the relationship by pushing away the person with whom they are making a connection.

The average Four's response is to take their feelings and emotions to yet another level, but it's hard on relationships when feelings appear to have no boundaries. When Fours don't know how to handle their full expression of feelings—happy, sad, and everything in between—those in relationship with them tend to pull back or withdraw. Unfortunately, the great fear of the Four is abandonment, so when people give pause or seem to go away, it justifies the Four's belief that they are unworthy of both love and relationship.

THE PATH TOGETHER

My friend Elizabeth who you heard about earlier shares life with her husband and children in Austin, Texas. Elizabeth is a portrait painter. Her canvases are large and her portraits are alive with vibrant color and exquisite detail. When I sit in front of one for a time, I can walk away almost feeling like I've met the subject. The evening Joe and I went to Austin to view her show was an extraordinary experience because it seemed to me that my friend's way of seeing the world was hanging on every wall.

As we entered the gallery, we were greeted and given a copy of "The Artist's Statement." At the top of the brochure it said:

What we have loved, others will love,
and we will show them how.

WORDSWORTH

What followed was Elizabeth's reflection on what was happening around the globe while she was painting—her responses and her hopes:

My work, in a general sense, is an often futile but ravenous and utterly unfulfillable desire to remain wide awake. Wide awake to what is around me and who is around me—mainly for the desire to find beauty—not just beauty in the sense of glamour or prettiness, but beauty as Baudelaire puts it as "the correspondent of Heaven." Jacques Maritain says, "Our love is caused by the beauty of what we love." I think I go around subconsciously constructing a world that is easier for me to love and therefore fosters more of it. Patty Griffin sings about being a servant of love, and we all are, it is just our choice as to how keenly we want to feel this. In the face of beauty, love is more easily present. In the construction of beauty, we are participating in the correspondence with eternity. And I'm not saying that the work is where the beauty necessarily lies. I'm saying that the intention of finding it in the other person is where the beauty lies. To fall in love with a person requires first that we perceive their beauty and that perception is dependent on the quality and the intentionality of our seeing. We must occupy ourselves to occupy the other.

Or, as e.e. cummings puts it: "To become an artist means nothing, whereas to become alive; or one's self, means everything."

Later on when I discussed the statement with Elizabeth, I said, "You know not everybody wants that, right?" And together we laughed.

When Fours trust the relationship, they can accommodate your awareness of their uniqueness without feeling that their authenticity was sacrificed.

RELATIONSHIPS *for* FOURS

After all is said and done . . .

Fours have the gifts and the grace to hold both beauty and pain without the need to choose one over the other. For those of you who are Fours, you will have to allow the idea that you are flawed in some significant way to fall by the wayside. Here are a few other suggestions for Fours:

You can . . .

- surround yourself with beauty—but not all the time.
- bear witness to pain without having to fix it.
- learn to seek normalcy inside expectations of the exceptional.
- create your own image and express yourself in manifold ways. But not everyone will approve or understand. And that's okay.

But you can't . . .

- live an exceptional life based on fantasy.
- have lots of people who can accommodate your emotional volatility.
- have more than one or two people who are able to give back in equal measure what you are willing to put into a relationship.

So you'll need to accept that . . .

- people might actually understand you and like you. It could be that you are lovable and that you are enough.
- life is ordinary, and that's okay.
- there is no such thing as a perfect relationship. Perfection lies in your ability to accept what is and make it into something better.
- most people don't value authenticity in the same ways that you do.
- you're going to have a few deep and significant friendships rather than lots of shallow, social relationships.

Fours need trust and steady attention in their personal relationships. They want you to be authentic with them—any suspicions of pretense may cause them not to trust you. They will generally prefer fewer mutually loving, one-on-one relationships to lots of social contacts. People who do not shy away from their intensity (and in fact value it), who are calm even when the Fours are volatile, and who cultivate mutuality will find Fours to be wonderful friends. Here are some other things to keep in mind:

- Don't be afraid to tell Fours when you feel pressure to be more than you can be or to handle more than your part.

- Fours need to be both unique and authentic. That will require some compromise at times. If you can be honest about how their style affects your life, the differences can be managed.

- Fours long for what they don't have, and they are comfortable with longing. It's not something for you to fix.

- It is very important that you tell Fours how their mood changes affect you.

- Don't tell Fours to "cheer up." They are usually neither sad nor depressed. Fours are comfortable with melancholy. But remember it's okay for you to be lighthearted.

- If you can learn to model balance and stay present when they are caught in a cycle of moodiness, it will be a tremendous gift.

- Fours don't like accusations (perhaps none of us do). Don't accuse them of being too sensitive or of overreacting.

- Fours feel like they aren't good enough or aren't liked, and they need you to acknowledge their feelings. Affirm that the feeling is valid for them without affirming the premise it is based on. Remind them that you see them as someone more competent, valuable, and lovable than they are seeing themselves in the moment.

- In the workplace, set clear expectations, trust them to do their own work, give them creative freedom, and recognize their strengths and abilities.

- Don't take the pull-push dynamic personally. Allow them room to process their feelings.

5s

MY FENCES
HAVE GATES

*A*s I was entering the grocery store, I noticed a voicemail from my friend Carolyn. "Hi, I was hoping to catch you. I'll just try to call back later. Hope you're having a good day." Carolyn and I have been close friends for forty-eight years, but she rarely calls. She works at our ministry center, so if she calls about business and I don't answer, she leaves a detailed message. I listened to the brief voicemail again and I was sure something was wrong.

Carolyn is ten years older than I am. I met her when I was in college, and we worked together for most of fifteen years.

When I phoned, she answered on the first ring.

"Hey, I got your message, are you okay?"

"Well, you know I finally went to the doctor a few weeks ago. I'm okay. At least I think I am. The doctor sent me for a mammogram. A few days later, she called to say I needed to schedule another one because of a suspicious spot. I did and there are actually two spots, so I have to go in for another test that should be more conclusive."

Carolyn has always been hesitant to share things that are personal. My mom was a Five and the same was true of her. I've often wondered if it's because a Five doesn't want to have to manage any feelings other than their own. So my daughters and I always listen carefully for even a hint that all is not well in Carolyn's life.

Carolyn continued, "I've been planning to tell you and the girls. I thought I would just tell the one I talked to first. But I went to the movie with Joey the other night, and we were having such a good time I didn't tell her. I told Jenny this morning so I thought I'd better call you."

This woman has been my best friend for all of my adult life. She has never married, and although she has her sister, niece, and nephew, we consider her part of *our* family. I didn't want her to go in for her test alone, and *I* wanted to go with her— remember, I'm a Two. So I said, "Okay, well, as soon as I get home I'll send you my travel schedule and you can work with it so I can go with you for the next procedure." I always try to be respectful of her need for space and privacy, but I also don't want her to face difficult experiences by herself.

Sometimes when I insist on being with her, she thanks me for being there and admits that she's glad she's not alone. But this time Carolyn said that she would be fine and that she is "saving me for the big stuff" when she *really* needs me. I explained that there is enough of me to be with her for this *and* the big stuff.

"I'll be fine. Really, there is no need for you to go. Now I've got to get to work. I love you, love you, love you!"

Aware that when she said, "I love you" three times the focus had shifted to me, I told her how thankful I am for her in my life and I headed into the grocery store.

What's Going on Here?

Which person in the story do you identify with? Why?

How would you handle a similar situation with a close friend who is going alone to an important procedure?

In the context of friendship, what solution would honor both people?

How does the Enneagram explain what's happening here?

The Enneagram teaches us that there are nine fairly predictable ways of dealing with crisis. Fives are in the Fear Triad on the left side of the Enneagram and they manage their fear by gathering information and knowledge. That information is usually shared thoughtfully and methodically. It's standard for them to withhold pieces of information, share their feelings with only one or two people, and manage their reactions with thinking. Although they are unique in their need for privacy and independence, Fives' boundaries do allow for the exchange of personal information, but only on their terms.

I've learned from Carolyn, my mom, and other Fives that most of their feelings are translated into thinking before they are shared. It's not that Fives are bereft of feelings, it's that they struggle to hold them long enough to articulate and share them with someone else. As a Two, I nurture feelings. I journal about them, share them with others, connect them to feelings I've had in the past, and keep them close. But in my friendship with Carolyn, the solution is not to meet in the middle. That's unrealistic and would look, sound, and feel inauthentic. Our challenge is to allow each other the room to deal with life in our own way, make space for our differences, and respect the needs of the other.

THE WORLD OF FIVES

Fives respond to life by asking, What do I *think*? That's a great response in moderation, but life presents itself to us in ways that sometimes require *feeling* or *doing* along with thinking. Joined by Sixes and Sevens, Fives manage everything in their heads. They prefer convergent thinking, which offers one correct answer, to divergent thinking, which allows for creative ideas that come from exploring many possible sources.

Their lives are well planned, and spontaneity is neither comfortable nor appealing. They usually have a predictable schedule, a chosen route to work that only varies when necessary, and an organized calendar. A morning routine might look like this: get up and brush teeth, open the blinds on the way to the kitchen, make the coffee and go to the front porch to get the newspaper, pour a cup of coffee and fix a piece of toast, read the front page of several sections of the paper, shower, make the bed, dress and leave for work at approximately the same time every day. With a schedule like that, imagine the challenge of integrating other people and their needs.

Relationships are risky for Fives. Nita Andrews, my friend who is a Five with a Four wing, explains it this way:

> The measured risk is what a Five is after. A *measured* risk. And then they test the waters and then they test them again. I don't know if it is nature or nurture. I'm not sure which came first, but I was an isolated child, so being underneath a piano and looking at the bottom of the keys—those little ordered, felt, off-white ivory pads— was comforting for me. My first painting, twenty years later, was of the underside of a piano. I lived under there as a child with a lamp and a book and a sheet over the piano. That was my fort for my Five-ness. I was already holding space for things and dragging them in, under my piano, for safe keeping.

But there's only room for one person under the piano. Getting the Five to emerge from that safety has conditions, so if you want time with a Five you will generally need to request it. An average Five will carefully evaluate the validity of your request and then weigh the time and energy it will take to accommodate it before responding.

Fives are often misunderstood by the Feeling Triad types—Twos, Threes, and Fours—who don't understand the need to assess time and energy in relationships. Relationships come naturally for feeling types, but not necessarily for thinking types, and especially not for Fives. Fives who are aware that they are often misunderstood would do well to spend some time explaining their way of seeing and sharing their needs early in the process of getting to know someone. Other people will have to learn that for Fives, time alone is a must if they are going to be comfortable offering themselves and their gifts to the world.

> The Enneagram doesn't just tell us who we are—it tells us who we can be.

INDEPENDENCE, PRIVACY, AND SELF-PROTECTION. We all avoid something, and Fives avoid being dependent on others. In fact, they over-value independence, so establishing and maintaining boundaries is second nature to them.

Because of this high value on privacy and independence, Fives have a limited capacity for interaction with other people, which is a significant obstacle in relationships. It also means they tend to struggle with having a limited amount of energy. This is tricky when it comes to getting to know someone. Keep in mind that Eights have more energy than any number on the Enneagram and Nines have the least, but Fives have an allotted amount of energy for every day, and when it's gone for that day, it's gone. It's like manna, the food provided for the Israelites wandering in the desert: they got enough for the day, but they couldn't store up the leftovers for tomorrow.

Fives see independence as the key to managing their lack of energy. This is ironic since the real solution is interdependence—real, authentic relationship—but that requires an understanding about relationship that most Fives don't have until midlife. In fact, one of the reasons Fives avoid needing help from others lies in the reality that they find interaction to be a challenge. Older Fives tell me they wish connecting with other people could be easier. They share that they missed a lot in life because of their need for time alone and the space to process thoughts and feelings privately.

Social conversations that include where we live, what we do for a living, what we think about the weather, and which sports teams we support are comfortable topics for Fives. However, when it comes to a narrative about their personal lives or their views on a timely or controversial subject, Fives tend to withdraw. One Five recently said to me, "I don't offer my thoughts or my story to many people. It's about preserving my privacy." Sharing personal details takes more energy and leads to more questions, all of which the Five experiences as draining.

> **5** Fives are great listeners because they are interested in anything and everything, and they have no desire to be the center of attention.

Fives manage both their privacy and their independence in many ways, some intuitive and some intentional. One Five taught me the value of compartmentalization when he said, "I would be hesitant to introduce the people I work with to my friends from church. And my friends that I work out with have never met my family. They all know me in different ways and they know different things about me. And I like it that way." But it can be challenging for relationships to accommodate a strong desire for independence and a deep commitment to privacy. Both have value, but too much of either is a problem.

AVARICE. Now there's a word we don't use every day. In general usage *avarice* means greed, but as the passion for Fives, it has to do with believing that they don't have enough inner resources to meet the demands of life, including relationships. Their greed is for privacy and independence.

We know from Enneagram wisdom that our passions teach us lessons we need to learn. Many relationships are built around an exchange of ideas or expertise, and some of our closest connections are the result of having a need and allowing someone else to meet it. So the commitment of Fives to provide everything for themselves hinders their ability to connect with others. Relationships are enhanced when Fives can hear and consider ideas or solutions that differ from their own, and when they can accept help from someone else.

Fives often look at life through a lens of scarcity: they withhold their resources so their needs will never present a problem for someone else. But this kind of thinking inhibits the seeking and building of relationships. The idea that your needs are going to be a problem for the people who love and care about you is simply not true. The vulnerability of need is one of the ways we learn to love, but it has to be a two-way street.

DISCONNECTION FROM DOING. Along with Fours and Nines, Fives are aware when a situation calls for action, but they are often blind to the possibility that they should be the one to act. They may wonder what happened, analyze how it should be fixed, or suggest ideas to others, but they rarely take initiative to *do* something. One result of this lack of initiative is that they repress their ability to affect the world. But it's a cycle: Fives believe that they do not or cannot make a difference, in either process or outcome, so they don't take action. And then this inactivity feeds into their mistaken beliefs that they have no power to effect change.

This thinking has serious implications for relationships since it means that Fives often don't do their part, ignoring responsibilities at work and at home. On a deeper level, those of us who love Fives struggle when they are unwilling or unable to act on our behalf when we need them most.

STRESS AND SECURITY

Singer-songwriter Michael Gungor, who is a Five, explains the Enneagram this way: "The Enneagram is not about a pigeonhole, it's more like 'here's a place where you hover' and you can see how stress is affecting you and you can see possible indicators about what you could do to alleviate the stress. That is very helpful, especially in building relationships." I like his "here's where you hover" language because it describes the dynamic nature of the Enneagram.

Fives tend to like the Enneagram when it comes to movement in stress and security, since they move to Seven when they are feeling stressed and to Eight when they feel secure. Unequivocally, I would say these are among the strangest moves on the Enneagram, and if they aren't understood, they cause big problems in relationships.

When Fives are in excess in their number, their world becomes smaller and smaller. They become less concerned about the needs of others and more concerned about themselves and their overwhelming desire for privacy and security. And when the world of a Five is shrinking, there is

5s and Others

1s: Fives tend to struggle with the Ones' desire for perfection —the criticism of Ones often makes Fives feel inadequate and incompetent. But the standards of Ones are not a reflection of the competency of Fives, and Ones can really benefit from the objectivity of Fives.

2s: Fives have a hard time with the effusive affection of Twos. The Two's way of being in the world seems like a waste of energy to a Five. But Twos are good social models for Fives—they can help others feel wanted and at ease, and they learn to honor personal boundaries.

3s: Threes are busy with their own lives, so they don't require too much from Fives. But Threes care a lot about image and what other people think of them, and that is seldom a main concern of Fives. Fives have a gift to offer Threes in teaching them the value of withdrawing.

4s: Perhaps the most challenging personality type on the Enneagram for Fives is Fours since they are opposite in many ways. But if (or when) Fives develop a Four wing, they will find that the connection of head and heart is a real asset in relationships.

5s: Fives are most comfortable with other Fives, but the connection may only involve thinking. The challenge is to use thinking, feeling, *and* doing.

6s: The loyalty of Sixes is a gift for Fives, but social anxiety in Fives can be exacerbated by a Six who is in unfamiliar territory. A good exchange is if the Five can be rational about a Six's unwarranted fears, and if the Five lets a Six help plan solutions for situations that make them anxious.

7s & 8s: Fives share a line with Sevens and Eights on the Enneagram. Eights learn from Fives the value of pulling back, observing, thinking, and then reconnecting. And Fives offer Sevens a chance to find balance between participation and observation. Sevens offer Fives a lightheartedness that can keep them from taking themselves too seriously. And Eights help Fives define what they like or want.

9s: Nines are a challenge when they don't just go along with what Fives think. But that's good for Fives. Nines may ramble a bit, but in important matters they are independent thinkers. And it's a gift that they don't pressure Fives to do things they don't want to do.

essentially no room for other people. One of my students who is a Five said, "When I'm overwhelmed, either in emotional or dysfunctional situations, I just evacuate." But Fives may need to resist this tendency at times for the sake of relationships.

In stress, Fives intuitively take on some Seven behavior. This is quite a change since they tend to be self-conscious and self-contained most of the time. If Fives can learn to aim for the healthier side of Seven when they feel stretched and overwhelmed, they find some freedom to lean into what others think or suggest as a path forward. When they're focused outside of themselves, they have more fun, they're less restrained, they are more comfortable in the world, and they find more comfort in the company of others.

Fives are prone to what the rest of us call "dry humor." Sometimes this humor is too cynical or sarcastic and it creates misunderstanding, especially with the feeling types. But with some influence from Seven, Five humor is softened in a way that allows connection with others. Both the humor and the connection are revealing and appreciated.

A relationship also has to be able to accommodate a secure Five in Eight space. Fives in Eight are much more spontaneous and outspoken, more connected to their feelings, and less afraid of activity. Life and relationships seem to offer more abundance when Fives enjoy some Eight energy. In this space, Fives invest more in others and receive a greater return, dispelling the myth that giving and connection will always be too costly.

Fives tend to maintain the status quo: they avoid change and risk, and they manage both their fear and their limited energy with restricted involvement in the outside world. These choices limit their opportunity for accessing both Seven and Eight energy, which can be a loss for Fives and for their relationships. When they find comfort with more spontaneity and a little more risk there are payoffs both for them and for others. The ability to move to the stress number is good for relationships in every Enneagram number, and it's especially good for Fives.

LIMITATIONS IN RELATIONSHIPS

It would be wrong to say that Fives don't need and want relationships. They do. However, they are most comfortable with just one or two close friends outside of family. In fact, sometimes they experience people as intrusive.

Years ago, when my children were small, Carolyn went camping with us for the weekend. On the way home I noticed her in the rearview mirror looking both tired and pensive. I asked what she was thinking about. She said, "Honestly, I was just thinking about how much I'm looking forward to being home and by myself!" I think Fives get lonely just like the rest of us, but I also think their need for connection is more easily met.

The behavior available to us in times of stress and security can be incorporated into the whole of our lives.

It helps to keep in mind that Fives have to be willing to choose participation over observation. A pastor who is a Five says, "Being in vocational ministry, my challenge is about how to encounter the world while learning to initiate and engage reality. In my second half of life, I've actually been mistaken for an extrovert a few times. I think it's because I've learned how to be 'on' and present. Most people don't know that I have to recover from doing that—the next day I need to spend the whole day alone just to recharge my batteries."

For Fives, relating to people is costly. It is not uncommon for them to need an entire day of solitude after being available and present to others. This time serves more than one purpose. As organized thinkers, Fives need time to process their experience in relation to what they already hold to be true.

My friend Carolyn doesn't like the idea of most social gatherings, but once she gets there she seems to have a good time. I asked her once how she manages and she said, "I have a magic shield. When I get too uncomfortable, I put it on."

I appreciate this mental image and understand that it allows her to participate without having to expend precious energy. But I was curious about how the shield works, so I decided to conduct an experiment: I challenged Carolyn to come to a fellowship supper at our church and wear her shield. Her instructions were to come to the dinner, bring a dish, sit and eat with a group of people, and then leave for home. I would then work the crowd asking if anyone had seen her. She did. And I did. And not one person said they saw her. Not even the people she sat with while she ate.

Since then, I have become more aware of the people who come to me with questions at events who I don't remember seeing in the audience. These individuals are almost always Fives. It seems that Fives can hide in any group, whether it be seven people or seven hundred.

But Fives miss out when they hide, and other people miss out on knowing them. It is brave of Fives to show up—more brave than for any other number. What many of us give from our excess, Fives give from their

> Because Fives are so private, they often refuse much-needed help—even from the people who love them most.

substance. Even still, Fives should risk being known. They are sure to discover that the mutual benefit in the relationship outweighs their personal cost.

THE PATH TOGETHER

Kenny is an Anglican priest and a friend. He describes the delight of growing up as a Five in Oklahoma:

> When I was a child, one of the greatest gifts my parents gave me was a set of *World Book Encyclopedias*. Every day before school, even before breakfast, I woke up and I picked a letter and I read from the encyclopedia. It was an aesthetic experience for me—it gave me joy. There was a sense of connection, a kind of an inner beauty, to what I would learn. Moving on to late elementary school or middle school, my mother got me a chemistry set. I went to the library and checked out books of chemistry experiments. My dad worked for Philips Petroleum Company in the oil business in Bartlesville, and he would bring me used chemical apparatuses from their lab. I had a chemistry lab in my garage—it was great!

Just when I thought I'd heard it all, Kenny added a PS: "Oh, and I collected maps from service stations."

While Kenny paints a charming picture of his childhood as a brilliant, introverted Five, it's important to understand the distinction between being introverted and being inaccessible. Fives have an unexpected capacity to bring delightful curiosity to the moment and the relationship. Their independence may appear impassable, but those fences have gates.

RELATIONSHIPS *for* FIVES

After all is said and done ...

Enneagram wisdom teaches that Fives are the only number capable of true neutrality. That's a gift to offer others. Here are some other things for Fives to keep in mind:

You can ...

- survive being seen and known before you are completely ready.
- have lasting friendships that are filled with soft and subtle experiences of familiarity.
- find measured ways of being in the world that don't deplete your store of energy.
- be in an intimate relationship without risking more than you can stand to lose.

But you can't ...

- live your life without needing help from others at times.
- be competent in all areas of life all the time. The need to learn is not incompetence, it's inexperience.
- have healthy relationships without risking giving up some of your time, letting go of some of your privacy, and finding a way to offer and receive affection.
- know everything.

So you'll need to accept that ...

- relationships will require more or less from you depending on the seasons of life. You will have to give more in midlife than will be required in the final third of life. And because of grace, you will have what you need.
- although you value thinking over feeling and doing, that is not true for many of the other people in your life. In order to connect with others, you will have to work to balance your thinking with some emotion and action.
- the outer world has value that extends far beyond gathering information.
- relationships can't always be on your terms—the needs of others are as real and pronounced as yours.

Fives measure life's events by how much it will cost them in terms of money, energy, time, privacy, and affection. Fives usually don't know what to give so they hold back. If you can be aware of that, you can let them know that you notice when they give something without being asked. In a relationship with a Five, also keep in mind:

- Be clear with Fives about what you need and want, but don't be demanding.

- Be aware that Fives don't always pick up on innuendo and indirect suggestion in conversation.

- Be forthright and direct with Fives, but don't use too many words.

- If you have a problem with a Five, agree on a time to discuss it. Give the Five time to think about your concern and then limit the length of the conversation. Good language would be, "I want to tell you what I want and then you can tell me whether you can give it to me."

- If you're in a relationship with a Five, don't push them to socialize with other people. That has to come naturally for them; they don't do well when pushed.

- Fives have trouble finding their place in what is already happening. You can help by saying, for example, "Would you like to sit with us? We have an extra chair." Follow that with an introduction like, "Hey, everyone, this is Tom. We work together."

- If you ask a Five what they feel, they will tell you what they think. You will have to be persistent to move a conversation to the feeling level.

- Incompetence and inadequacy are central to the Five's fear. There is probably never an appropriate time to discuss either one lightly.

- It is very important for Fives to know what is expected of them. They like details.

- Fives have a strong desire to live life so that they never have to depend on someone else to take care of them. If they are in a position where they need your care, offer it with as few words and as little fanfare as possible.

6s

QUESTION EVERYTHING

*T*wo of my favorite musicians and favorite people are Sixes. Seemingly similar on the outside, Jill and Dana are so different. Jill lives in Nashville with her musician husband and their three beautiful children. One afternoon as Jill and I sat and sipped on their screened-in porch, she described for me what it's like to be a Six and a talented performer living and working in a town like Nashville.

People here have a vision. They have *their thing* that they do. Being a Six in Nashville is good for me because I don't need that—I don't need to have my own vision or my own thing. I'm happy to come alongside other people and support their vision, and when I walk off stage after doing that, I'm super happy.

There is a David Wilcox quote that my husband and I have identified with over the years: "When you go to a pop show, they're trying to convince you that they're different and that they're special, while folk musicians are trying to convince everyone that we're all the same." Our position has always been that we're the same. We're not special, we're not different, we're just like you. So, when I walk off stage, I don't want people to think I'm awesome or amazing. I want to be able to talk to them about their lives and their kids and tell them about mine. I really want them to know I'm just like them.

Jill's approach to her work is very different from Dana's. Dana is the director of the music and arts department, working with all ages in both choir and drama, at a big-steeple church in downtown Dallas. When I asked Dana why she became a leader, she smiled brightly and leaned forward with a ready answer about how choir was her "thing" in high school. Encouraged by her choir director, Dana started to explore using her gifts this way and was surprised by what she discovered:

Soon I found that I enjoyed helping others find their voices and I was able to help them be better together. I also discovered that I could make my choirs sound good by quickly diagnosing and fixing problems. And I was the leader so I could control the environment—literally. I make sure the temperature is controlled and that seating and lighting are appropriate. I see to it that the music is prepared, that the schedule is set and everyone knows what it is, and that the chosen repertoire is appropriate. And, this is really important, I also systematically create a climate of welcome, teamwork, and respect.

These two women, who are both performance artists and who are the same number on the Enneagram, are different from one another in ways that are subtle but significant.

What's Going on Here?

Which person do you identify with most—Jill or Dana? Why?

Look back at David Wilcox's quote about pop and folk musicians. Do you resonate more with folk musicians or pop musicians? Why?

Assuming musical talent isn't an issue, what would be comforting for you about being in Dana's choir? What would be uncomfortable?

How would you describe Jill and Dana's differences based on these two stories?

Sixes are the only number that can be divided into two types. The distinction between the two has to do with the way they respond to fear or anxiety, which according to Enneagram wisdom is their sin or passion. In response to fear, the motivation for Sixes is to *feel* safe and to *be* secure.

THE WORLD OF SIXES

The two types of Sixes differ by how they manage fear. Jill is a *phobic* Six. She is comfortable being one of a larger group since she is more focused on how we are the same than how we are different. She's interested in building relationships around common interests, she downplays anything that makes her stand out, and she has a gentle way of being with others—regardless of who they are. Jill likes structure that is familiar and rules instituted by someone else that are proven to be tried and true.

Dana is a *counterphobic* Six. She likes to provide security for others by creating structure where people can gather and feel safe. She thinks of every detail, she's comfortable being the leader and is more mindful of difference than sameness, she's interested in building relationships with and among people by helping them work together, and she is systematic in creating a community where everyone will know "how we do, what we do, and why." She stands out in a group and she finds a way to have an encounter with others—regardless of who they are.

Sixes are involved in more group activities than any other number on the Enneagram. Of the nine personality types, they are the most concerned about the common good. They are the glue that holds together all of the organizations that we belong to—they don't leave over minor conflicts and they don't move from group to group. Sixes are loyal, consistently striving to do their part, and they want to be part of something that is bigger than they are.

Both Jill and Dana are building community. As Sixes, they are both committed to creating open space and a safe place for everyone. But their ways of achieving this goal are subtly yet profoundly different: Jill *allows* community to form, and Dana *creates* the community.

THE NEED TO FEEL SAFE. Each type's passion (or sin) and their way of seeing the world can sometimes be so strong that it determines their choices. Sometimes, the passion is just an obvious expression of nonproductive behavior. At other times, all Enneagram numbers can lose themselves in its grasp. This is especially true and important for Sixes: their passion is fear, and that can escalate exponentially in a myriad of ways.

It is a fascinating exercise to watch both the local and the national news from the perspective of each number. It is a powerful experience to attempt to take it all in from the perspective of a Six. For them, every news event has a threatening element, creating a need for a plan.

It doesn't stop with the news. Commercials play on our anxieties and distrust, and all of this is exaggerated for Sixes. When I watch advertising on television, I might as well give up. I don't have a Bowflex machine. My dishwasher will catch fire any day now. The glass in the shower door is evidently *very* dangerous. I've been using the wrong toothpaste since I learned to brush. I need to lose weight, but how would I know which system to go with—Nutrisystem, Weight Watchers, Dr. Oz's two-week Rapid Plan,

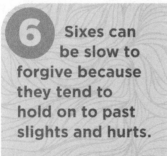

6 Sixes can be slow to forgive because they tend to hold on to past slights and hurts.

Jenny Craig, or Bistro MD? There is no possible way we've saved enough for retirement. Termites are eating our home from the inside out. And all pork is bad. Or is it chicken? Or beef? And to top it off, the organic vegetables aren't organic. Wow.

We all experience fear in ways that are associated with our types. As a Two, I am afraid people won't want me. Nines are afraid of conflict. Eights are afraid of being controlled. But for Sixes, fear itself is the preoccupation, and they are always asking, "What if?" Phobic Sixes tend to give in to fear. They are more malleable in relationships with people who are aggressive and sure of themselves. Counterphobic Sixes try to overcome their fears. They are distrustful of people who have too many answers and come on too strong, so they tend to want to find their own way. And many Sixes are a combination of both phobic and counterphobic depending on circumstances.

A phobic Six explains his type this way:

I have struggled with fear and anxiety my whole life, even since I was a little kid. I remember lying in bed worried about my pee-wee soccer game the next morning. *Pee-wee soccer!* I knew other kids didn't feel the same way—they just rolled out of bed and ran around the field. The funny thing is that I always played well. In fact, I was able to play so well over the years that I earned an athletic scholarship, so all that worry was just a bunch of wasted energy. As time went by, I got better at managing my fears, but they're always with me.

Now take a look at how my friend Sheryl, a counterphobic Six, describes her fears:

> I like to speak in public and teach, and I know other Sixes who are the same way. Though we have fear, it's not usually of social situations but of what-ifs. The scenarios our minds develop are about what could go wrong in novel situations. For example, if I know I have to teach or speak, I prepare thoroughly and don't worry much about it. I know I can do it. If I don't have time to prepare and I have to perform on the spot, I do it, but I have some anxiety about it.

Both are anxious, but phobic Sixes give in to their anxiety and get lost in imagining all the ways the worst could happen, while counterphobic Sixes expect the worst and expend the same energy making a plan for it.

We all have a strong need for control when we're afraid, but other numbers don't share the same *need* to feel safe. Sixes appreciate order, plans, and rules because they all provide a modicum of security. We feel safe when there is little or no chaos, when life is running smoothly and things are happening like they're supposed to. But relationships are messy—they have far too many variables to always run smoothly. So there are times when a Six's need to feel safe trumps relationships.

Sixes want predictability and hope for certainty, and they cannot count on either. Like Eights, they want to affect others without being affected or influenced in return, and that seldom happens. When they can't manage their anxiety, Sixes sometimes resort to leaning on the belief systems of the organizations they belong to. A Six told me, "I think we sometimes misplace trust—especially in leaders who we think can take care of us and make us feel less afraid. And then loyalty makes it hard to stop trusting, even if it's the wrong person." So Sixes can benefit greatly from learning to trust *their own* experience of life. They have a tendency to sell themselves short, and in doing so they place too much hope in others. And when Sixes don't trust themselves, everybody loses.

Discernment is usually more reliable when we give consideration to the entirety of our relationships. It's damaging, regardless of Enneagram number, when we get lost in the highs and lows.

PLANNING FOR THE WORST. Sixes manage their anxious feelings by imagining the worst thing that could happen and then planning for it. They try to be aware of and prepared for everything that could go wrong so they can be safe. I asked a friend who is a Six what it's like for her to travel.

> Because they often overthink, Sixes are prone to procrastination, but to others this can appear as a lack of commitment.
>
> **6**

As a traveler, I'm a great companion because I constantly scan for clues—which air terminal for the flight, where to catch the Metro or a bus, how it works to go to a bank or store in a foreign country. My huge antennae pick up clues and my mind analyzes quickly, so I can figure out and solve problems and get us where we need to go. Scanning is a habitual response to life. Sixes are always looking for hidden danger so we can deal with it.

Other Sixes choose to travel to a place that is familiar, where there are fewer variables and less to plan for. They might go to the same campground every summer, where they can reserve their favorite cabin in advance. Once they've become familiar with the town, where to buy groceries, safe places for the kids to play, and opportunities for recreation for the whole family, they can plan their time without having to include those variables and unexpected changes.

> **Each number's passion or sin can sometimes be so strong it defines their behavior.**

For family members and friends who are not Sixes, safety while on an adventure might not be the number-one concern. I suppose it's obvious that all numbers react differently to being away from home. For example, relationship problems are usually diminished when a One goes on vacation because they are more relaxed and less compulsive. But problems are exacerbated when a Six travels. Sixes have told me many times that protection is a core need they have in relation to those who are close to them. You can see, then, how when they are away from their normal routine they might be overprotective (phobic) because the routine is abnormal and there are so many unknowns. On the other hand, counterphobic Sixes have no patience with your fear unless you are willing to try to overcome it, so vacations are a great arena for that conversation to take center stage.

DISCONNECTION FROM PRODUCTIVE THINKING. Sixes struggle with the Enneagram teaching that they are "thinking repressed." They cannot imagine how that could be true because to them it seems that they are thinking *all the time*. But much of their thinking is not productive: it doesn't move them to action or insight. I know a successful executive nearing retirement who is a counterphobic Six and explains this kind of thinking:

> We are really up in our heads *thinking*. It's my favorite thing to do. I often say, "This does not make sense," which means I have apprehended it through my mind and it doesn't add up. That's usually fine except when the not making sense involves feelings, my own or others'. I can usually move on only when it feels safe,

Sixes ask a lot of questions— others can feel threatened when questions are too many, too personal, or too soon.

6

like it won't create problems, and when I've antici-
pated possible outcomes.

Sometimes I get tired of overthinking, and I act im-
pulsively. I've learned that I take action as a way of
stopping thinking, which sometimes works out and at
other times doesn't. It can be hasty and ill-considered,
which I hate because I believe I should have thought it
through better.

Sixes readily embrace the concept of thinking more productively, but they often don't know where to start.

There are certainly Enneagram numbers that find a lot of
comfort in plans and routine and predictability. But some
don't. For example, Nines can easily fall into a routine and
stay there without giving much, if any, thought to what might
go wrong. Fives like routine because it helps them manage
their limited amount of energy. Sixes not only like routines, they
find safety in them. But what about numbers who don't want life to be
so predictable? For some numbers,

Some Enneagram numbers prefer routine and others are energized by the unexpected.

freedom is as necessary to them as security is to Sixes. Many
relationship problems are rooted in this difference between
needing stability and thriving on spontaneity.

There is no problem with Sixes using thinking to gather information from the world. The problem begins when they react
too quickly and fail to use clear thinking to process information.

Sixes can add to the goodness of their relationships whenever they stop, breathe, and think clearly before falling into the trap of anxiety. Sixes make up things when they become anxious and then react to the story they have manufactured. Those who share life with Sixes find this pattern to be quite disconcerting, and Sixes must make a conscious effort to work on the discipline of waiting before responding.

STRESS AND SECURITY

When stressed, Sixes respond first by pulling back, and then by checking what they are thinking or feeling with people they trust because they often don't trust themselves. If you are in relationship with a Six who is stressed and they trust you, they will ask what you think is an appropriate response to their anxiety. Be sure to offer the best you have, but don't attach value to whether the Six follows your advice. Sometimes they will, but often they will not. Sixes almost always have an

6s and Others

1s: When Sixes are in a relationship with a One, their anxiety is often increased because they never feel good enough. This needs to be acknowledged and discussed, otherwise the One will feel like they are alone in trying to get things done.

2s: The Six's goal will almost always be about safety while the Two's goal will always be relational, so they'll need to agree to be honest about their differences. Additionally, Sixes should be careful about doubting the Two's motivation for what they do with and for others. Meanwhile, the Two needs to avoid focusing on the mistrust of Sixes. It can be messy.

3s: Threes love success and they trust it, but Sixes don't. Sixes will have to teach Threes about the anxiety that often accompanies their success.

4s: Sixes employ worst-case scenario planning, whereas Fours are comfortable with longing. Fours can get caught in "If only . . ." thinking, and the Sixes ask "What if . . ." questions. Watch for that.

5s: Fives don't need to have all the answers, so Sixes will have to work with them on fielding all their questions. Both are in the Head Triad and have a lot in common—and both can work toward adding feeling and doing to their thinking.

6s: With two Sixes, when one is afraid the other almost always responds with optimism, sort of like two kids on a seesaw. It's pretty great.

7s: Sevens go into their heads and imagine the future better than it will be. Sixes go into their heads and imagine it worse. Both can learn to use this dynamic to their advantage in relationships.

8s: Sixes and Eights are significantly different in that Eights move "too fast" for Sixes and Sixes are "too slow" for Eights. A value they share is loyalty. However, Sixes need to be careful since sometimes they are loyal to a fault.

9s: Sixes and Nines are fairly comfortable together because they can each see themselves in the other. Each will need to take responsibility for setting their own goals—waiting for suggestion or direction from the other is not the best course of action, but supporting one another will be fulfilling.

idea or a plan of their own, so when they question other people, they are just gathering information to see if it supports or discredits the decisions they've already made.

When I was a child, we made paper chains out of strips of construction paper for the Christmas tree. We cut the strips of paper, then glued them into interlocking circles. This is what Sixes do with fears and memories, past hurts, and disappointments: if a Six is afraid you are going to leave the relationship, they chain that feeling to everything that has happened in their life to make them fear abandonment. Relationships sometimes collapse from the weight of this chaining. But if Sixes can identify this pattern, they can stop doing it. It's worth the work both for the Six and for those they love.

When Sixes are stressed, and they've exhausted what chaining has to offer in terms of alleviating their concerns, they take on the behavior of a Three. In that move, they become more sure of themselves—they make decisions and take action, and there is much less second-guessing about their choices.

When Sixes feel like they are on top of things and life is going well—when they are experiencing security—they have access to some of the ways Nines inhabit the world. It's a beautiful thing when Sixes are able to trust themselves and their own experience of life, and it's good for their relationships. Sixes in this space have a sense that everything is going to be okay.

LIMITATIONS IN RELATIONSHIPS

Sixes are sincere in their desire to always do their part, but sometimes they fail to honor their priorities because they underestimate the time required to manage responsibilities and commitments. So it's a good idea for Sixes to estimate the time commitment for something and then double it. This helps them to honor their primary commitments to the people they love the most.

Another struggle for Sixes, even in their closest relationships, is to forgive and forget. They tend to believe that they can protect themselves by remembering hurts and disappointments, so forgiveness is difficult because it makes them feel both vulnerable and powerless. I've heard of Sixes who keep journals that track when someone they are in a relationship with hurt them—one woman even notes painful disconnections on a calendar, keeping those calendars year after year. Sixes need to learn that we will always fall short in relationships, forever working through disappointment with others. Even though this is more difficult for some Enneagram numbers than for others, we all need to give *and* receive forgiveness. It's just part of the deal.

For understandable reasons, Sixes find it hard to trust, but relationships can't survive without it. It is surely incumbent on the people they love to be honest and loyal and worthy of trust, but there is also work for Sixes to do: sometimes trust is a decision.

A couple came to see me a few years ago looking for a way to move forward in their relationship and believing the Enneagram could help. I wouldn't say their relationship was in trouble—they were just stuck. She had been married previously to a man whose abuse took the form of neglect. So by the time she divorced, it was hard to trust anyone, until she met the man who sat beside her in my office. They were very much in love, and they worked hard at having a healthy marriage and family life, but she was insecure and afraid to really trust both him and their love. As often as twice a week, she would start to worry that he was going to leave her. Of course, he had absolutely no intention of leaving and was hurt she would suggest that he might.

Sometimes trust is a decision.

As I listened to their story, I decided to share with them that Joe and I had a similar challenge early in our marriage. The turning point came when Joe held my hands and said, "I'm not leaving. I love our life. I love you and the children with all my heart. I am here and fully committed and fully engaged. So there is nothing else I have to offer. This work is on your side of the fence. You will either decide to trust that, or not. But there is nothing else I can do."

I decided to trust that promise.

THE PATH TOGETHER

Aware that many of his parishioners were Sixes, my husband, Joe, used Enneagram wisdom when leading congregations toward change. When remodeling a building or purchasing or selling church property, he knew that Sixes would need time.

Sixes hold together all of the organizations that we belong to and don't leave over minor issues. They're happy to do their part for the good of the entire community, but they want to be informed and they want to have a voice in decisions that affect them. Although Sixes have a lot to offer, they hesitate to speak up in real time because they don't trust themselves. They need time to process what they hear, formulate questions they might want to ask, and evaluate whether their questions or concerns have value for the entire community.

So for the good of all, Joe held every meeting twice. Twice. This afforded Sixes the necessary time to fully participate in the process. So by the time the second meeting rolled around, these individuals were prepared to ask well-thought-out questions, offer meaningful observations, and confidently contribute to the decision at hand.

It's believed by many that there are more Sixes than any other number, so it is sometimes difficult in our fast-paced society to accommodate their numerous questions and varied concerns. However, Sixes are the people most concerned with the common good and, when given time, Sixes see things that the rest of us miss.

We can all benefit from slowing down and viewing the world through the eyes of a Six.

RELATIONSHIPS *for* SIXES

After all is said and done ...

Remember that since we can't change how we see, we need to adjust what we do with how we see. For Sixes, there is no doubt that other numbers on the Enneagram don't struggle like you do with fear. Here are some other things for you to keep in mind:

You can ...

- learn to trust yourself, but only if you practice. Some things can be learned only by experience.
- learn to trust your inner ways of knowing.
- listen to your body. Your head and your heart will lie to you but your body will not.

But you can't ...

- expect others to be as loyal and faithful as you are to the groups you both belong to. The way they handle their commitments and responsibilities is not within your purview.
- be noticed without taking some risk. Some say that Sixes just want to blend in. I don't think that's true—I think you do want to be noticed, but you aren't always willing to take the necessary risk.
- always feel safe, but you can recognize when fear is becoming self-indulgent.

So you'll need to accept that ...

- some things *will* work out, and if they don't, you will have everything you need to address whatever situation arises.
- fear has played a role in your life. But you can also begin to diminish that through awareness and by working on productive thinking.

RELATIONSHIPS *with* SIXES

The main thing to keep in mind in relationship with a Six is that trust is a big thing for them. They tend to create boundaries to keep out the untrustworthy, so they ask a lot of questions to get more information. And when they get more of the right kind of information it's very reassuring, which leads to more trust. Here are some other things to consider:

- Sixes have a deep appreciation for people who are both genuine and authentic, but they don't trust appearances. They watch to make sure you are who you say you are.

- Worst-case scenario planning is comforting to Sixes, so take them seriously when they talk to you about what could go wrong. Telling them that they don't need to worry and that everything is going to be fine will feel patronizing, disrespectful, and dismissive. But do focus on the best possible outcome instead of the worst.

- Encourage Sixes to trust themselves more and to take more (measured) risks.

- It doesn't help to just say things like, "You should trust yourself more." It does help if you take the time to point out to a Six some previous times when they did trust their own ideas and their own ability to carry them through without checking with anyone else.

- At home Sixes need emotional attentiveness and conversation. They need someone who is a partner in the everyday details of life.

- Sixes like friends who are emotionally mature, honest, and not too needy.

- Sixes often keep their anxiety to themselves. They usually try to manage it alone so they aren't making it a big deal for anyone else.

- Sixes require a lot of reassurance—observable and verbal—about your commitment to them.

- Encourage Sixes to act when they are overthinking. They tend to confuse thinking about something with doing something about it.

- Point out all the good things they bring to a relationship.

- Be kind and thoughtful when answering all of their questions.

7s

IT'S ALL GOOD

*W*hen Darrin was a junior in high school, he and three of his friends were involved in a late-night adventure at a popular lakeside park that included lots of fun and laughter, a lack of clothes, and some beverages that were not allowed by his parents or the law.

Darrin was one of those kids who always got caught. In fact, his parents often received a call about what he was up to before he got home. Such is the nature of being the preacher's son in a small town. On the rare occasions when Darrin didn't get caught, he usually told on himself simply because he had a hard time not sharing his delight in his adventures.

And this time his dad was *very* unhappy. It wasn't as much about the lakeside caper as it was about including three boys from their congregation. After an initial confrontation about Darrin's poor choices and lack of regret, the two of them stopped talking to one another. Darrin did not apologize, his dad would not budge until he did, and his mom was stranded somewhere in the middle.

Finally, after three or four days, she caught Darrin between school and baseball practice and told him to go to the church and apologize to his dad or surrender the keys to his truck. After some pushback he said, "Okay, I'll go. But I don't understand apologizing. I love Dad more than anybody—you know that. I would never offend or hurt him on purpose, so why do I have to say I'm sorry? It wasn't about him. It was all about me and my friends. No one got hurt and no damage was done."

She simply held out her hand and said, "Go apologize or give me the keys. You may not understand the need for apologies now, but you will someday. Consider this a practice run."

As he headed to the door he said, "I don't have much time. It will have to be quick."

She shot back, "With you, if it's not fun it's always quick, so that won't be a surprise."

Several years later, when Darrin was away at college, the phone rang at 2:30 a.m. His mom answered with her heart pounding in her chest. It was Darrin, asking her to get up and go to the kitchen so she'd be wide awake for what he wanted to tell her.

"Darrin, how could I not be awake? Are you okay? What's wrong?"

He answered, "Mom, I need you to teach me again about apologizing. I can't remember much about what you said when

Dad and I weren't speaking after that night at the lake. I need help! I'm pretty sure if I don't apologize now, Traci is going to break up with me. What should I say? How do I start?"

What's Going on Here?

Which person in the story do you find it easiest to identify with—Darrin, his dad, or his mom? Why?

Why do you think Darrin struggled to understand how his actions negatively affected others?

What was Darrin's motive for apologizing to his dad? To Traci?

How does the Enneagram explain what's happening here?

Darrin is a Seven on the Enneagram. All Sevens are motivated by a need to be happy and avoid pain. Immature or average Sevens often dismiss the importance of emotions in themselves and in others. They see the world as their playground, and they are happiest when they are on the move, enjoying life, and going from one activity to the next. They'd rather not deal with anything unpleasant or uncomfortable.

This preference for the lighter side in Sevens leaves them with a half range of emotion, and that can be a deal breaker in relationships. It's important to give this imbalance some serious consideration. If Sevens aren't willing to acknowledge their discomfort with feelings that are heavy or sad, it can be costly. Healthy interpersonal dynamics are the cornerstone of a good relationship, so the agendas and feelings of others can't be ignored—something average Sevens are prone to do.

This inability or unwillingness to appropriately deal with feelings is problematic. When others can't be honest with Sevens about what they feel and what they need, the delayed emotional responses are usually expressed as anger, shame, fear, or perhaps resentment, all of which are damaging to relationships. If Sevens do the work of paying attention to and bringing up feelings, it saves a lot of pain in the relationships that mean the most.

THE WORLD OF SEVENS

Sevens are typically energetic and charming people. But they can sometimes overvalue their own charm. They avoid limitations—especially those imposed by someone else—and they avoid direct confrontation. Using humor and intentional distraction, they can slip away from trouble almost without being noticed. When Sevens do anything out of a sense of duty, their lack of enthusiasm is palpable; they are present, but they hold back on their energy waiting for some future event that is more promising. Each of these characteristics can cause problems with others.

7 It's a challenge for Sevens to acknowledge and take full responsibility for their part in conflict without assigning blame to others.

Mihee Kim Kort, a writer and Presbyterian minister, shared some of her challenge as a Seven married to a Six.

"He needs routine," she explained. "That rubs off on me. I can see how it's helpful for the kids. I try to be consistent, but it never works out. I pick them up after school and we go with whatever the weather is, what they're feeling. We may go straight to a playground or to the library, but we try to stay out as long as possible."

But then she told me she feels guilty about staying out. "Maybe the kids do need to come home. Maybe they need a place to rest and decompress by just watching a little TV. I personally just feel like for *my* sanity, *I can't go straight home.* Being cooped up in the house with a lot of screaming, a lot of chasing, and a lot of negotiating is really hard for me."

Every Seven I know has a big heart: they are generous and willing to make sacrifices for those they love. But more than any other number I think they feel trapped, caught between their seemingly endless need for stimulation and the needs of others. Listen closely and you will hear a lot of Sevens say, "I want to do *whatever* it takes for you to be happy." And they mean it, but they don't want to lose themselves in the process. Sevens generally have long lines of suitors who feel ditched by them, who took the relationship more seriously than the Seven did. It's easy to misunderstand the boundaries Sevens have in relationships.

> The Enneagram helps us to identify our blind spots when it comes to dealing with our feelings and the feelings of others.

One of the limitations Sevens struggle with is time. I recently heard a Seven say, "I wish there were two more days in the week. Just two more days." They never seem to have enough time to do all the things they have planned or want to do. And all the projects they didn't finish serve as reminders that time is running out.

Sevens think and then they do, without even a nod to feelings. They have to be taught to consider the feelings of others and the consequences of their behavior. And then they have to learn what to do with those feelings, theirs and others'.

A PASSION FOR PLEASURE. In their constant pursuit of pleasure, Sevens are anxious to fill themselves up with positive, stimulating experiences. Simply stated, they want more of whatever pleases them. This is also known as gluttony, which is the Seven passion. Although gluttony has a negative connotation, in this case it refers to the constant desire for more. All of us are trying to fill an inner emptiness, and we all try to fill it in different ways. When discussing her understanding of gluttony, Shauna Niequist admits, "My appetites—I think maybe I feel them more strongly than other people do."

Shauna recognizes the effect that her Seven nature has on her relationships—both good and bad:

Part of why I love the Enneagram is that recognizing that I'm a Seven helped me understand that the best parts of me and the worst parts of me are not just a random collection but they're very related to each other. So I love to do a million different things. I love for life to be full of variety. I'm terrible at routine. I want everything to feel like a special occasion. I want more of everything. *And* I can run myself ragged trying to have too much fun. The people around me can be worn out by my enthusiasm. Understanding those things as related and part of a whole was really, really helpful for me.

Other people can't be you.

On the other hand, if I'm not feeling well or if something's going on—if I'm only running at half energy for whatever reason—people notice that and they say, "What's wrong with her?" There's an expected level of energy that people want me to bring into a room. In working with that for the last couple of years I've come to understand that bringing my whole self doesn't always mean bringing my most wound-up self.

When they experience frustration or feel needy, Sevens intuitively start moving, seeking external gratification. Part of their journey toward transformation involves changing that pattern of behavior and turning inward. While effective for the Seven, it is disconcerting for those who have come to rely on the Seven's playful energy.

REFRAMING AS SELF-PROTECTION. Although many numbers fear being abandoned and alone, Sevens are totally afraid of being trapped and engulfed, so they find an escape route in reframing. They intuitively reframe feelings of pain and failure almost immediately as something else. Our oldest son, Joel, was a basketball player in high school and college. He is 6'3" and wears a size fifteen shoe. Suffice to say, he is a good playmaker but he's not fast; he can jump, but not very high. One night after a high school playoff game, Joel spoke up from the back seat. "Hey Mom, did you catch us with that killer dunk before halftime?"

"I caught the dunk, but who is 'us'?"

"You know: *us!*"

Recalling that Joel had been on the bench for "their" awesome dunk, I was aware, again, of my Seven son's vivid imagination and his natural ability to reframe his experiences. Sevens change sad feelings into something more positive easily and quickly. With some maturity, they are able to hold sadness or fear before remaking the experience into something that is more comfortable. But until then, they repress sad or negative feelings. Those feelings don't completely go away. In fact, they resurface at unpredictable times in the future.

Their ability to reframe and rename what's happening allows Sevens to move to a magical place in their heads that has been serving them well since they were children. Joel has a story about the day he got lost at Six Flags when he was five. "The policeman who waited with me at the security tower told me everything would be fine, and I believed him. So I just closed my eyes and used my other senses to *imagine* that I was riding the rides, eating ice cream, and laughing and playing with my sisters. Honestly, I had a great time." Every Seven that I know has their own story about the first time they experienced being able to refocus their attention away from fear or sadness toward something much more wonderful and safe.

But reframing and refocusing can lead to significant problems in relationships, since other numbers don't have this magical gift. When something in the lives of other numbers makes them sad or feels threatening, their response is different from the Seven's. And out of frustration, these numbers may label a Seven's reframing of any negative into a positive as immature, irresponsible, and unrealistic. Often, in such circumstances the

7s and Others

1s: Sevens can learn from observing Ones in relation to boundaries, self-control, and completing tasks. Ones can benefit from the lightheartedness and spontaneity of Sevens. It's a good exchange.

2s: Sevens need a lot more freedom than Twos. In relationships, Twos will need to be more trusting and Sevens will need to work on sharing their plans: where they'll be, what they'll be doing, and when they'll be available.

3s: Sevens and Threes need to be aware of a difference that might be mistaken for sameness. Sevens don't like to limit personal options. Threes don't like to limit how many hours they will work. This one is tricky—it requires being intentional about communication.

4s: Fours and Sevens are more alike than we might think. In fact, it's very difficult to tell them apart as children. But they present as opposites in adulthood because of their respective emotional preferences. Fours see the glass as half empty; Sevens see it as half full. If they are willing to honor their differences while trying to bridge them, they have a lot to offer one another.

5s: One of the reasons Sevens and Fives can so successfully connect is that they share a line on the Enneagram. That means they can each see themselves in the other. Both appreciate adventure and are easily bored with repetition—that's a good place to keep coming back to.

6s: In looking to the future, Sevens and Sixes usually see things differently. Sevens tend to imagine it better than it will be, while Sixes anticipate it being worse than it will likely be. Both can benefit from a more balanced perspective of the future.

7s: Sevens fear commitment, routine, and predictability. Sevens in relationship with other Sevens will find limitations challenging.

8s: Sevens think and then do. Eights do and then think. Be careful with this dynamic in relationship!

9s: Sevens and Nines offer one another a unique kind of balance because Sevens love options and Nines find too many choices to be paralyzing.

relationship begins to look and sound like a parent and child relating to one another. It's probably disrespectful on both sides, and the only solution is intentionally choosing to meet in the middle.

A SMOKESCREEN OF ACTIVITY. Sevens avoid pain of all kinds, but especially the pain of being trapped in the predictability of a routine. The thought of emotional or physical pain that can't be managed or controlled is almost unbearable, and they don't know how to make life work in a relationship with someone who can't or won't be happy.

Sevens are with Fives and Sixes in the Fear Triad on the Enneagram, and they most fear being trapped with anything unpleasant. One of their ways of managing this fear is to keep their options open—it's part of their understanding of abundance. The idea of a stable, secure, measured day-to-day life is a turn-off for them. They want to participate in as many activities as possible, even ones that aren't on the schedule. But enjoyment of these activities with others is compromised when about halfway through one event, Sevens start to think about what's coming next.

Relationships require commitment—not just commitment to stay connected and work things out, but to smaller, seemingly less important agreements like being on time, finishing what you start, and honoring a plan even when a more exciting opportunity presents itself. Once Sevens commit (which has to be their idea) they are all in. The challenge is to define with other personality types what "all in" means. Think about it. For Ones and Eights, "all in" means hanging in there from start to finish. And for Twos, "all in" includes being *in* emotionally. These are important distinctions in relationships. Sevens like being in a relationship with people they love, and they are devastated when relationships end. It would be a misunderstanding to think that endings are easy for Sevens. Quite the opposite is true.

THE NEED FOR OPTIMISM. A Seven's need for optimism is directly connected to their desire to believe that the world is safe, people are good, and their needs will be taken care of. So it's hard to remember that Sevens are in the Fear Triad since most Sevens we know don't seem fearful. In fact, they appear to be cheerful and upbeat and fun. Young Sevens sometimes say to me, "How can I be right next to Six on the Enneagram? I don't have anything in common with Sixes." Richard Rohr says, "Optimism and pessimism are surprisingly not far from one another: both are intellectual mechanisms for managing the abyss and dangers of life."

A woman recently shared with me what she believes Sevens can offer our world:

> I think we're living in a time where we need some healthy optimism. We need some dreamers—some people who aren't afraid to dream bigger dreams. I'll be one of the first to criticize or be critical of someone who is tone-deaf or blind to racial or gender issues. But at the same time, I don't want people to be stripped of their bigger visions for community, and being together, and their belief in what love does when it's allowed to flourish in our communities. As much as people might think I'm being naive and superficial, I still want to hold on to the possibility of hope and joy.

We sometimes miss the good that Sevens have to offer our communities and our relationships because we fail to take them seriously. Their optimism is necessary.

STRESS AND SECURITY

When Sevens are at their best they are ambassadors for hope. They are lighthearted, generous, caring, and creative, and we all benefit from seeing the world through their eyes. But at their worst, they can be opinionated and stubborn. Along with Threes and Eights, they need to remember that when they are absolutely sure they're right, they're probably wrong.

When life is particularly stressful, every number exhibits excessive behavior associated with their personality. It's not pretty in any of us, and in Sevens it becomes frenetic activity that has the potential to undermine their true desires. Thankfully, stressed Sevens have easy access to behavior associated with Ones. With the mature side of the perfectionist influence, Sevens slow down and are more discerning about what they will do, with whom, and when; they are less selfish and more likely to finish things they've started. It's a good move for them, and it's particularly good for their relationships. One of the common complaints about Sevens is that they don't follow through, so when they do, it provides healing. Another complaint is that they don't pay attention to details, but in the One space, they do. And when they access One behavior they find a necessary balance, at least for a time, between dreaming and doing.

When Sevens are more secure, they can use Five energy and behavior as a model for stepping back from too many interests and too much activity with too many people. Then they are able to give time to only one or two relationships, or they can focus on a few things instead of many. Sevens

> **Sometimes the enthusiasm of Sevens is misinterpreted as a desire to impose their will.**

7

tell me that this is where they experience the most satisfaction, and yet it only works for a limited time. One Seven
told me that unless she is influenced by the move to Five, she
doesn't make room for quality time with significant others.

Awareness of differences helps us in limiting what we
expect from others—and that's a really good thing. Others
cannot see the way you see. I have learned from teaching in
the recovery community that expectations are resentments
waiting to happen. It's smart to keep that in mind when it
comes to building and maintaining relationships.

LIMITATIONS IN RELATIONSHIPS

Sevens repress feeling, attempting to always keep themselves
in the happy range. As much fun as that can be, it's a significant limitation when you consider that the other eight
numbers are managing life with a full range of emotion.

The Seven's charm is more effective professionally than in
relationships. They have to learn that in interdependent relationships they're not the CEO—other people don't have to
agree with what they say or do what they want. And interdependence is good for all of us, so Sevens need to learn to
moderate their ego, at home and at work.

Sevens believe their needs are simple and few, when in reality they are complex people with complex needs. Many of
them struggle with how things can be great one moment in a
relationship, and problematic the next. They don't like it when

things are emotionally messy—and relationships are notoriously messy. Sometimes with Sevens the problem is getting them to see and admit that there is a problem. Then comes the challenge of dealing with it. So Sevens need to learn to deal with problems as they arise, setting aside their wish that problems would fix themselves. Repairing a significant breach in relationships with those we love the most requires a tenacious maturity that many Sevens have to work to develop.

THE PATH TOGETHER

On *The Road Back to You* podcast, Shauna Niequist, who loves to gather people in her home, responded to our question about how she had used the Enneagram as a tool in her spiritual life:

> The most helpful thing for me in learning the spiritual aspect of the Enneagram was giving myself permission to not do it the way the Fours in my life do it. My mom and my husband are Fours. They are both introverts. They're deep thinkers and deep feelers, and they're contemplative by nature. I'm a party-thrower by nature. That looks a lot less spiritual to a lot of people. But I would say the first thing was giving myself permission to not be like a desert mystic and instead to offer my greatest gift, spiritual or not, which is hospitality.
>
> I think it's one of the ways God uses my life, and I have a disproportionate amount of joy when I practice

hospitality. It makes me unreasonably happy. If I sell X amount of books, I'm like, "That's good," but a really meaningful dinner party is like, "I believe in God and I believe He's good." That really means something to me.

By refusing to seek fulfillment by any path other than their own, Sevens model for us the satisfaction that's possible when we acknowledge the inherent value in our uniqueness.

That kind of uniqueness needs to be honored and celebrated.

RELATIONSHIPS *for* SEVENS

After all is said and done . . .

Sevens struggle more than any other number to accept that there is a limit to what they can have. And it's an even greater challenge for them to accept that there are some things they just can't have, no matter how hard they try. It has been very helpful for the Sevens I know to learn and commit to a contemplative practice such as meditation or centering prayer. Beyond that, as a way to stop frenetic thinking and planning, it will be helpful if Sevens can learn to use this mantra: *It is what it is.*

You can . . .

- live into the reality that the growing edge for you will always be where there is pain that cannot be reframed or renamed. You can learn what it has to teach you.
- dream new dreams, but they won't always come true.
- have a life that is filled with abundance and joy, but you won't recognize it if you don't also experience scarcity and pain.

You can't . . .

- manage life with a half range of emotions—and you can develop the other half.
- be responsible and dependable while keeping your options open. You can make dependability one of your options.
- get where you want to go with excessive behavior. You can moderate your way of being in the world.

So you'll need to accept that . . .

- sometimes life is boring, and there is no way for you to reframe that. You just have to live through it.
- relationships are as valuable for personal growth as they are for enjoyment.
- people may presume that you don't go deep because you're interested in a lot of things.
- your behavior is often both alienating and charming at the same time.
- the avoidance of painful, personal feelings doesn't work well in a long-term relationship.

RELATIONSHIPS *with* SEVENS

In my experience, when Sevens really begin to work on themselves, the people around them are quick to say, "What happened to you? You used to be so much fun." Those of us who love Sevens need to be careful that we don't expect them to show up with behavior we've asked them to moderate. Here are some other things that will help grow your relationship:

- Don't try to get Sevens to commit to specific routines and schedules. They need spontaneity and flexibility.

- Sevens need the other person in the relationship to have his or her own energy and interests. Don't depend on Sevens for constant companionship.

- When criticism is necessary, be gentle and brief.

- If you want to *share* your feelings with a Seven, by all means do that. But do not *process* your feelings with a Seven. You will need to do that with someone else.

- Sevens love to be with people, and they really value time alone. It will help if you contribute to making both happen.

- It's not helpful to talk to a Seven about their potential. They don't respond well to expectations, and any talk of potential feels wrapped in expectation.

- One of the best gifts you have to offer a Seven is encouraging them to allow and experience a full range of emotions.

- Most adults who are not Sevens have forgotten how to play. Invite a Seven to teach you about the gift of playing.

- Sevens need the space to freely express their ideas. If you decide to go a different direction, that's completely okay with them.

- When Sevens really want something that is within your purview to give them, they are very persistent. It's like being pecked to death by chickens.

- Be attentive to their stories. The telling of their stories is often the way they express and share their feelings.

CONCLUSION

When I was a little girl, my parents had a small library in an upstairs bedroom, which was home to my brother Carroll when he had polio and to my Grandpa Brown when he was dying. Neither could get out of bed, so I entertained myself and them by serving as their librarian, reading to them and listening as they read to me. They were both very sick. Honestly, I've wanted to write a book that would heal people for as long as I can remember.

In those same years, I dreamed of a day when I would get married and have children and live happily ever after. Life is seldom that simple. I was a divorced mom with three children when Joe and I married. He adopted the children, and we had a fourth. We've worked hard at figuring out how to live together, love each other well, and keep each other forgiven and free.

We've known the Enneagram for most of our thirty years together, and it has made an enormous difference for us and for our family. Truthfully, I cannot imagine our life without it. But it's just one of the many practices that help us in our search for understanding who we are and who we can be when we are loved, accepted, and safe. It is my hope that you will use the Enneagram to offer love and acceptance and assurance to those people who inhabit your days and your life.

I wrote this book for anyone who wants to do better at being in relationship with others—at home, at work, at church, or with friends. And I've tried to be clear without becoming simplistic. I'm sure you understood it—even the parts you didn't like.

I want it to make a difference. But that isn't up to me. It will be up to *all* of us

- to protect our relationships from anger, fear, and shame;

- to be compassionate when we see others struggling to think productively, act intentionally, and feel deeply; and

- to take seriously what others say about how they experience us in relationships, and then use what the Enneagram teaches to do something about it.

Perhaps we could agree that in those moments, when we are healthy enough and mature enough, we will do what we can with what we know *for the good of all.*

ACKNOWLEDGMENTS

When it comes to the Enneagram, my teachers are everywhere. They are in the classes I teach and the audience when I speak. They are in the airport when I travel, in our church when I worship, in the grocery store when I shop, and in my neighborhood when I come home. They are all people who are making their way through the world doing the best they know how with what they have and how they see, and I owe them all a great debt.

Most of all I want to thank my husband, Joe Stabile. His unending commitment to me and to our life together is both honoring and challenging as he continues to insist that we commit ourselves to the work we are called to. Our children and their husbands and wives, along with our grandchildren, are my motivation for wanting to do my part to make the world a better place. I am so grateful for all of them. Thank you, Joey, Billy, Will, Sam, Jenny, Cory, Noah, Elle, Piper, Joel, Whitney, Joley, Jase, B.J., and Devon for oh so much! Saying yes to this meant saying no to you more often that I would ever want to.

Father Richard Rohr invited me into the study of this ancient wisdom, so whatever my teaching has become is easily traced back to him.

I am so grateful for my friend and literary agent, Sheryl Fullerton. She is the best of the best, and I can't imagine this book without her influence on every page.

There are no words to adequately thank the men and women who have been in my Apprentice Program for the past nine years. They have taught me so much of what I know to be true about the Enneagram. I am grateful beyond measure for the thousands of people who have shared their weekends and their stories with me over the past twenty-eight years. They are the reason the information I have gathered about the Enneagram became wisdom.

Special thanks to my editor, Cindy Bunch. She helped me find my way in a world that is relatively new. This book is better because of her encouragement and her unending patience with me. And to Jeff Crosby, unending respect and gratitude. The staff at IVP is a gathering of men and women who are smart and creative and so good at what they do. Thank you to Elissa Schauer, Ben McCoy, David Fassett, Dan van Loon, Rebecca Carhart, Andrew Bronson, Alisse Wissman, Krista Clayton, Justin Paul Lawrence, Marty Schoenleber, and everyone who works there—from the front desk to the warehouse. What a gift to work with these consummate professionals who also happen to be really good human beings.

There are so many people who give their time and energy to the work of Life in the Trinity Ministry: Carolyn Teel, my best friend for forty-seven years; Mike George, Joe's best friend for fifty-two years, and his wife, Patsy; Ann Leick, Cindy Short, B.C. and Karen Hosch, Dr. John and Stephanie Burk, Tanya Dohoney, John Brimm, Tom Hoekstra, Jane Henry, and Luci Neuman, who dreamed of a future for LTM that we could hardly imagine. Dr. Shirley Corbitt and Marge Buchanan, thank you for being a witness to all of my adult life. Joel Stabile and Laura Addis, I cannot imagine my work in the world without your gifts and talents. Dr. Bob Hughes, thank you for insisting that I believe I am wanted.

Special thanks to Jim Chaffee and to Jana Reiss. And also to Meredith Inman and Corey Pigg for all you do on my behalf.

I am, and have been, well loved by many people who encourage me to live my life well and to do what is mine to do in regard to teaching the Enneagram. To each of you, I am so very grateful.

I want to acknowledge and express my thanks to those who have led the way for me as I have studied the Enneagram. Their insights make this wisdom more accessible for all of us.

Richard Rohr, OFM

Claudio Naranjo

Renee Baron

Elizabeth Wagele

Andreas Ebert

Don Riso

Russ Hudson

Helen Palmer

David Daniels

Virginia Price

Beatrice Chestnut

Kathleen Hurley

Theodore Donson

Thomas Condon

Susan Reynolds

Ian Cron

Sandra Maitri

Lynette Sheppard

Suzanne Zuercher, OSB

Clarence Thomson

Margaret Keyes

Roxanne Howe-Murphy

NOTES

EIGHTS—VULNERABILITY IS NOT WEAKNESS

20 *Vulnerability is the idea*: Brené Brown, "The Power of Vulnerability," TED Talk, www.ted.com/talks/brene_brown_on_vulnerability.

33 *The way the church runs*: Nadia Bolz-Weber, "Find Power in Vulnerability: An Interview with Pastor Nadia Bolz-Weber, Enneagram 8 (The Challenger)," *The Road Back to You* podcast, episode 3, July 17, 2016.

NINES—RISKING CONFLICT FOR CONNECTION

39 *The greatest things*: Andy Gullahorn, "The Enneagram in Marriage with Andy Gullahorn, Enneagram 9 (The Peacemaker), and Jill Phillips, Enneagram 6 (The Loyalist)," *The Road Back to You* podcast, episode 29, March 22, 2017.

44 *I have struggled to find*: Chris Gonzalez, "The Enneagram and Therapy—A Dialogue with Chris Gonzalez, Enneagram 9," *The Road Back to You* podcast, episode 24, January 18, 2017.

45 *When I understand that*: Mike McHargue, "Learning to Express Confidences About the Things You Believe: An Interview with Science Mike, Enneagram 9," *The Road Back to You* podcast, episode 5, July 26, 2017.

52 *When I am sharing*: Gonzalez, "Enneagram and Therapy."

ONES—THINGS COULD ALWAYS BE BETTER

60 *The main thing about*: Christopher and Amanda Philips, "When Good Enough Is Never Good Enough: A Conversation with Christopher and Amanda Philips, Enneagram 1," *The Road Back to You* podcast, episode 12, September 21, 2016.

TWOS—YOUR FEELINGS OR MINE?

80 *the inability or unwillingness to*: Don Richard Riso and Russ Hudson, *The Wisdom of the Enneagram* (New York: Bantam Books, 1999).

THREES—BEING EVERYONE BUT MYSELF

108 *the saddest number on the Enneagram*: Richard Rohr and Andreas Ebert, *The Enneagram: A Christian Perspective* (New York: Crossroad, 2001), 85.

FOURS—GO AWAY BUT DON'T LEAVE

121 *I wish that for*: Bob Dylan, "Positively 4th Street," *Positively 4th Street*, Columbia, 1965.

FIVES—MY FENCES HAVE GATES

136 *The Enneagram is not about:* Michael Gungor, "Finding Your Place in the World: An Interview with Michael Gungor—Enneagram 5 (The Investigator)," *The Road Back to You* podcast, episode 7, August 10, 2016.

SIXES—QUESTION EVERYTHING

146 *People here have a vision*: Jill Phillips, "The Enneagram in Marriage with Andy Gullahorn, Enneagram 9 (The Peacemaker), and Jill Phillips, Enneagram 6 (The Loyalist)," *The Road Back to You* podcast, episode 29, March 22, 2017.

SEVENS—IT'S ALL GOOD

169 *He needs routine*: Mihee Kim-Kort, "Processing Pain Through Optimism—Insight to the Enneagram 7 (The Enthusiast) with Mihee Kim-Kort," *The Road Back to You* podcast, episode 25, January 25, 2017.

170 *My appetites*: Shauna Niequist, "Savor Everything: An Interview with Shauna Niequist—Enneagram 7 (The Enthusiast)," *The Road Back to You* podcast, episode 6, July 27, 2016.

Part of why: Ibid.

176 *Optimism and pessimism*: Richard Rohr and Andreas Ebert, *The Enneagram: A Christian Perspective* (New York: Crossroad, 2001).

179 *The most helpful thing*: Niequist, "Savor Everything."

ALSO AVAILABLE

ALSO AVAILABLE

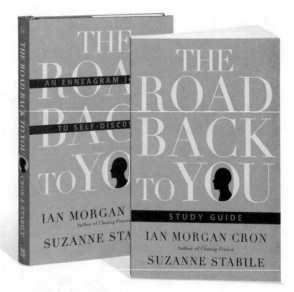

 **LIFE IN THE TRINITY**
——— **MINISTRY** ———

Drawing on timeless wisdom and the Living Word, Life in the Trinity Ministry is a community serving the Triune God and our brothers and sisters through study dedicated to encouraging self-knowledge and fostering spiritual maturity.

What does the Lord require of you but to do justice, and to love kindness, and to walk humbly with your God? Micah 6:8

> *The Enneagram: Know Your Number*
> Suzanne Stabile
>
> *The Enneagram: Wings, Stress and Security*
> Suzanne Stabile
>
> *The Aggressive Stance, The Dependent Stance,*
> and *The Withdrawing Stance*
> Suzanne Stabile
>
> *The Enneagram Journey DVD Curriculum*
> and *Participant's Guide*
> Suzanne Stabile
>
> *Centering Prayer*
> Reverend Joseph Stabile

For more information about Suzanne or any of these resources, go to lifeinthetrinityministry.com.

 .ivp formatio

BECOMING OUR TRUE SELVES

The nautilus is one of the sea's oldest creatures. Beginning with a tight center, its remarkable growth pattern can be seen in the ever-enlarging chambers that spiral outward. The nautilus in the IVP Formatio logo symbolizes deep inward work of spiritual formation that begins rooted in our souls and then opens to the world as we experience spiritual transformation. The shell takes on a stunning pearlized appearance as it ages and forms in much the same way as the souls of those who devote themselves to spiritual practice. Formatio books draw on the ancient wisdom of the saints and the early church as well as the rich resources of Scripture, applying tradition to the needs of contemporary life and practice.

Within each of us is a longing to be in God's presence. Formatio books call us into our deepest desires and help us to become our true selves in the light of God's grace.

VISIT

ivpress.com/formatio

*to see all of the books in the
line and to sign up for the
IVP Formatio newsletter.*